MOB RULE IN
NEW ORLEANS

ROBERT CHARLES &
HIS FIGHT TO DEATH,
THE STORY OF HIS LIFE,
BURNING HUMAN BEINGS ALIVE,
& OTHER LYNCHING STATISTICS

By

IDA B. WELLS-BARNETT

WITH
INTRODUCTORY CHAPTERS BY
IRVINE GARLAND PENN AND
T. THOMAS FORTUNE

First published in 1900

Read &' Co.

Copyright © 2020 Read & Co. History

This edition is published by Read & Co. History,
an imprint of Read & Co.

British Library Cataloguing-in-Publication Data
A catalogue record for this book is available
from the British Library.

Read & Co. is part of Read Books Ltd.
For more information visit
www.readandcobooks.co.uk

CONTENTS

MISS IDA B. WELLS (IOLA)

GENERAL NEWSPAPER CORRESPONDENT AND ASSOCIATE EDITRESS

By Irvine Garland Penn

That "perseverance overcomes all obstacles," is fully verified in the life and character of Miss I. B. Wells, who was born at Holly Springs, Ark., and reared and educated there. Her parents died while she was attending Rust University, which compelled her to leave school in order that she might support her five brothers and sisters, all being younger than herself.

She taught her first school at the age of fourteen, and with this work and journalism she has been an incessant laborer. She has taught in the schools of Arkansas and Tennessee, and has at various times been offered like positions elsewhere; but preferring to teach her people in the South, she has continued to labor there. For six years she has followed her vocation as teacher, in the city of Memphis.

During this time she began to write for the press. Her first article was a "write-up," at the request of the editor, of a suit for damages, in which she was the complainant. This paper was *The Living Way*, which she contributed to for the space of two years. This engagement introduced her to the newspaper fraternity as a writer of superb ability, and therefore demands for her services began to come in. T. Thomas Fortune, after meeting her, wrote as follows: "She has become famous as one of the few of our women who handle a goose-quill, with diamond point, as easily as any man in the newspaper work. If Iola were a man, she would be a humming independent in politics. She has plenty of nerve, and is as sharp as a steel trap."

She is now the regular correspondent of *The Detroit Plaindealer, Christian Index,* and *The People's Choice.* She is also part owner and editor of *The Memphis Free Speech* and *Head Light,* and editress of the "Home" department of *Our Women and Children,* of which Dr. William J, Simmons is publisher. Decidedly, "Iola" is a great success in journalism, and we can but feel proud of a woman whose ability and energy serves to make her so. She is popular with all the journalists of Afro-American connection, as will be seen by her election as assistant secretary of the National Afro-American Press Convention, at Louisville, two years ago, and her unanimous election as secretary of the recent Press Convention, which met at Washington, D. C, March 4, 1889. Miss Lucy W. Smith gives an account of the many papers to which "Iola" has contributed.

In summing up her character as a writer, we can but say "Amen" to what Miss Smith says of her: "Miss Ida B. Wells, "Iola," has been called the "Princess of the Press," and she has well earned the title. No writer, the male fraternity not excepted, has been more extensively quoted; none struck harder blows at the wrongs and weaknesses of the race.

"Miss Wells' readers are equally divided between the sexes. She reaches the men by dealing with the political aspect of the race question, and the women she meets around the fireside, She is an inspiration to the young writers, and her success has lent an impetus to their ambition. When the National Press Convention, of which she was assistant secretary, met in Louisville, she read a splendidly written paper on "Women in Journalism; or, How I would Edit."

"By the way, it is her ambition to edit a paper. She believes that there is no agency so potent as the press, in reaching and elevating a people. Her contributions are distributed among the leading race journals. She made her debut with *The Living Way,*

Memphis, Tenn., and has since written for *The New York Age, Detroit Plaindealer, Indianapolis World, Gate City Press, Mo., Little Rock Sun, American Baptist, Ky., Memphis Watchman, Chattanooga Justice, Christian Index, Fisk University Herald, Tenn., Our Women and Children Magazine, Ky.,* and the Memphis papers, weeklies and dailies. Miss Wells has attained much success as a teacher in the public schools of the last-named place." All in all, we are proud to own Miss Wells as our "Mrs. Frank Leslie."

A CHAPTER FROM
The Afro-American Press and Its Editors, Part Second, 1891

IDA B. WELLS, A. M.

By T. Thomas Fortune

One of the marvels of modern society is the honorable position which woman has secured in the affairs of mankind. She is no longer a cipher; she is a positive force. Regnant in the home, a co-ordinate force in the movements which make for human happiness, she must reckon in every accurate estimate of contention or achievement. In what manner she has arisen from the thralldom of ancient times is answered by the grasp which Christianity has secured upon a large portion of mankind. Only in Christian countries has woman secured a measure of equality with the forceful agents that make the world's history. In pagan countries she is still the idol of the harem or the beast of burden for the peasant.

It is a notable fact that in the anti-slavery struggle women contributed almost as largely as men to the moulding of public opinion necessary to the manumission of the slave. Women such as Lucretia Mott, Harriet Beecher Stowe, Sojourner Truth, Lydia Maria Childs, Anna Dickinson and others were towers of strength as well as inspiration. The work before the Afro-American, comprehending the intricate problems of his relation as a man and citizen, I feel safe in saying will never be performed as it should be until we have a race of women competent to do more than bear a brood of negative men. That such a womanhood, untainted by the horrible moral malformation and obliquity of slave masters, is already a possibility we have sufficient evidence.

Ida B. Wells, the oldest issue of James and Elizabeth Wells,

9

the subject of this sketch, was born at the beautiful town of Holly Springs, Miss., in the midst of a fateful epoch. Great moral questions were uppermost in the public mind and discussion. In the forum of public prints, in the homes of the slave-holding oligarchy, in the cabins of the haunted and oppressed slave, the one question uppermost in the minds of all was that of abolition of slavery. The immortal Lincoln had issued the most momentous proclamation ever promulgated by the chief executive of a great nation. The alarums of internecine strife were dying away in subdued echoes, in which the sorrows of a great people were commingled with abounding joys. It was a period in which it was well to be born, if a man is a product in the development of his character of contemporaneous as well as prenatal influences.

The subject of this sketch was precocious in the acquisition of useful knowledge. When the Freedmen's School was established at Holly Springs she attended it until the building of what was then known as Shaw, but was subsequently Rust University. In consequence of the death of both parents of yellow fever, within a day of each other, in 1878, she was under the necessity of leaving school for the purpose of undertaking the support and education of the five children, younger than herself, who had been so suddenly committed to her care. A greater responsibility could not have fallen upon shoulders so young and upon one less experienced as a bread-winner, for she had had indulgent parents, whose chief delight was to give their children all the advantages of school which had been denied them through a cruel and barbarous institution. How hard the task was and how well performed need not be dwelt upon here, further than to say that the two sisters are given every advantage possible in the way of education.

For three years she taught in the Marshall and Tate county public schools of Mississippi, attending Rust between the terms. She then went to Arkansas and taught six months in Cleveland county; then returned to Memphis and taught two years in the

Shelby county public schools, resigning to take a position in the Memphis city schools in the fall of 1884, which she held for seven years.

It was while teaching in Memphis that she began to write for the public press, appearing first in the Memphis *Living Way*, for which she wrote some time under the *nom de plume* of "Iola." She dealt mostly with some one or other of the phases of the race problem, and her views were widely quoted by other newspapers of the country. She became a regular contributor for the Kansas City *Gate City Press*, the Detroit *Plaindealer*, the *American Baptist*, the *Christian Index*, and other race papers. In June, 1889, she secured a one-third interest in the Memphis *Free Speech* and became its editor. Messrs. Nightengale and Fleming the former owners of the paper, continued the partnership until January 1, 1892, when Rev. Nightengale sold out to Mr. Fleming and Miss Wells.

Because of utterances of the Free Speech regarding the management of the public schools in 1891 the School Board decided that they could not employ so severe a critic; hence she was not re-elected to her position for the ensuing session of 1891-'92. She then gave her entire time to the paper, not at all deterred by the usual fate of race newspapers. She firmly believed that such a venture could be made to pay by first putting something in her paper worth reading, then taking steps to see that it was read by placing it in the homes of the people. She travelled extensively in the Mississippi Valley, from which she wrote graphic letters descriptive of the country and condition of the people. She went into their homes and not only learned of them but endeared herself to them as well. Her paper became a household visitor throughout the valley.

Few persons have brought more enthusiasm to their work than Miss Wells. She properly estimated the work of the race newspaper in educating the people to a proper conception of their rights and duties as citizens, and labored with an eye single to this object. The people seemed to feel the unselfish nobility and sustained it as they had never before sustained a newspaper. Of course it was natural that Miss Wells should take a strong stand against mob law. Many a sturdy blow she dealt upon the head of the gigantic monster. She felt that her life-work was in the South, where the vast majority of her people reside, and where she once expected they would always reside. At the highest point of her enthusiasm in the work, with prosperity crowning her labors on all hands, there came a rude awakening, a terrible shock, and the foundation of her confidence was destroyed forever. On March 9, 1892, there occurred in Memphis a tragedy which threw the whole city into a ferment of the wildest excitement and despair. Three reputable members of the race had been confined in the county jail for defending themselves and property from an attack by white ruffians masquerading in citizens clothes as officers of the law. Several of these ruffians had been wounded. A mob of white ruffians proceeded to the jail and securing the three Afro-Americans did them to death. Panic seized upon the people. Confidence in the legal machinery of county and State was undermined and many began to move away from the mob-infected city, encouraged thereto by the *Free Speech* and the ministers of the gospel.

After these brutal murders the white papers of Memphis, in the mad effort to placate the mob sentiment, teemed with the vilest utterances that ever disgraced the freedom of speech. They wrought the white masses to a state of absolute frenzy. It was in this state of the public temper that a paragraph in the *Free Speech* was taken by a daily paper and distorted into an excuse for calling on the white citizens to mob the proprietors of *Free Speech*. To this end a meeting was held. The business manager of the paper fled for his life, and Miss Wells, the editor, who was in Philadelphia at the time, was warned that she could not return to the city without danger to her life.

As in the old days at Alton, Ill., her splendid business was destroyed, the voice of a brave champion of right, justice and law was silenced in the home of oppression, and free speech, which

John Milton has made the heritage of Anglo-Saxon-speaking races, was strangled to death. The concerted attempt of many Southern white men to put a padlock on the lips of freedom of speech will prevail no more in the case of Miss Wells than in the case of Elijah Lovejoy at Alton, and of William Lloyd Garrison in Baltimore. The *Genius of Universal Emancipation* is the voice of God, and cannot be stifled. The suppression of Miss Wells' newspaper at Memphis possibly marked a well-defined period in the contention upon which we have entered to wrest from wicked men the justice denied us as men and citizens, and she should consider it an honor that such a calamity came upon her in the prosecution of a cause so sacred. No history of the Afro-American of the future will be complete in which this woman's work has not a place. From the vantage ground of New York, and associated with the *Age,* the splendid work she began in the South Miss Wells hopes to continue until the victory is won. The extensive statement made by her in the *New York Age* of June 25, 1892, of the reasons which led to the suspension of her newspaper, and as an exhaustive statement of the true causes of lynch and mob law, was one of the clearest, most convincing and most pathetic expositions of fact made in recent times to the voluminous discussion of the race problem. It created a veritable sensation, and was referred to and discussed in hundreds of newspapers and thousands -of homes. It is a historic document, full of the pathos of awful truth.

Although not a graduate, because of reasons previously stated, Rust University conferred upon Miss Wells the degree of Master of Arts at the commencement exercises of 1892.

As a writer Miss Wells lacks in the beauties and graces affected by academicians. Her style is one of great strength and directness. She is so much in earnest that there is almost an entire absence of the witty and humorous in what she writes. She handles her subjects more as a man than as a woman; indeed, she has so long had the management of a large home and business interests that the sharpness of wit and self-possession which characterize men of affairs are hers in a large measure.

Few women have a higher conception of the responsibilities and the possibilities of her sex than Miss Wells. She has all of a woman's tenderness in all that affects our common humanity, but she has also the courage of the great women of the past who believed that they could still be womanly while being more than ciphers in "the world's broad field of battle."

There is scarcely any reason why this woman, young in years and old in experience, shall not be found in the forefront of the great intellectual fight in which the race is now engaged for absolute right and justice under the Constitution. No other woman of the race occupies to-day a better position to do good work, or is more generously endowed to perform it. Strong in her devotion to race, strong in the affections of her people, and strong in the estimation of influential men, co-workers with her in the cause, with all the future hers, if she fails to impress her personality upon the time in which she lives, whose fault will it be?

A CHAPTER FROM
Women of Distinction, Chapter VII, 1893,
by L. A. Scruggs

INTRODUCTION

Immediately after the awful barbarism which disgraced the State of Georgia in April of last year, during which time more than a dozen colored people were put to death with unspeakable barbarity, I published a full report showing that Sam Hose, who was burned to death during that time, never committed a criminal assault, and that he killed his employer in self-defense.

Since that time I have been engaged on a work not yet finished, which I interrupt now to tell the story of the mob in New Orleans, which, despising all law, roamed the streets day and night, searching for colored men and women, whom they beat, shot and killed at will.

In the account of the New Orleans mob I have used freely the graphic reports of the *New Orleans Times-Democrat* and the *New Orleans Picayune*. Both papers gave the most minute details of the week's disorder. In their editorial comment they were at all times most urgent in their defense of law and in the strongest terms they condemned the infamous work of the mob.

It is no doubt owing to the determined stand for law and order taken by these great dailies and the courageous action taken by the best citizens of New Orleans, who rallied to the support of the civic authorities, that prevented a massacre of colored people awful to contemplate.

For the accounts and illustrations taken from the above-named journals, sincere thanks are hereby expressed.

The publisher hereof does not attempt to moralize over the deplorable condition of affairs shown in this publication, but simply presents the facts in a plain, unvarnished, connected way, so that he who runs may read. We do not believe that the American people who have encouraged such scenes by their indifference will read unmoved these accounts of brutality, injustice and oppression. We do not believe that the moral conscience of the nation—that which is highest and best among us—will always remain silent in face of such outrages, for God is not dead, and His Spirit is not entirely driven from men's hearts.

When this conscience wakes and speaks out in thunder tones, as it must, it will need facts to use as a weapon against injustice, barbarism and wrong. It is for this reason that I carefully compile, print and send forth these facts. If the reader can do no more, he can pass this pamphlet on to another, or send to the bureau addresses of those to whom he can order copies mailed.

Besides the New Orleans case, a history of burnings in this country is given, together with a table of lynchings for the past eighteen years. Those who would like to assist in the work of disseminating these facts, can do so by ordering copies, which are furnished at greatly reduced rates for gratuitous distribution. The bureau has no funds and is entirely dependent upon contributions from friends and members in carrying on the work.

IDA B. WELLS-BARNETT
Chicago, Sept. 1, 1900

MOB RULE IN NEW ORLEANS

SHOT AN OFFICER

The bloodiest week which New Orleans has known since the massacre of the Italians in 1892 was ushered in Monday, July 24, by the inexcusable and unprovoked assault upon two colored men by police officers of New Orleans. Fortified by the assurance born of long experience in the New Orleans service, three policemen, Sergeant Aucoin, Officer Mora and Officer Cantrelle, observing two colored men sitting on doorsteps on Dryades street, between Washington Avenue and 6th Streets, determined, without a shadow of authority, to arrest them. One of the colored men was named Robert Charles, the other was a lad of nineteen named Leonard Pierce. The colored men had left their homes, a few blocks distant, about an hour prior, and had been sitting upon the doorsteps for a short time talking together. They had not broken the peace in any way whatever, no warrant was in the policemen's hands justifying their arrest, and no crime had been committed of which they were the suspects. The policemen, however, secure in the firm belief that they could do anything to a Negro that they wished, approached the two men, and in less than three minutes from the time they accosted them attempted to put both colored men under arrest. The younger of the two men, Pierce, submitted to arrest, for the officer, Cantrelle, who accosted him, put his gun in the young man's face ready to blow his brains out if he moved. The other colored man,

17

Charles, was made the victim of a savage attack by Officer Mora, who used a billet and then drew a gun and tried to kill Charles. Charles drew his gun nearly as quickly as the policeman, and began a duel in the street, in which both participants were shot. The policeman got the worst of the duel, and fell helpless to the sidewalk. Charles made his escape. Cantrelle took Pierce, his captive, to the police station, to which place Mora, the wounded officer, was also taken, and a man hunt at once instituted for Charles, the wounded fugitive.

In any law-abiding community Charles would have been justified in delivering himself up immediately to the properly constituted authorities and asking a trial by a jury of his peers. He could have been certain that in resisting an unwarranted arrest he had a right to defend his life, even to the point of taking one in that defense, but Charles knew that his arrest in New Orleans, even for defending his life, meant nothing short of a long term in the penitentiary, and still more probable death by lynching at the hands of a cowardly mob. He very bravely determined to protect his life as long as he had breath in his body and strength to draw a hair trigger on his would-be murderers. How well he was justified in that belief is well shown by the newspaper accounts which were given of this transaction. Without a single line of evidence to justify the assertion, the New Orleans daily papers at once declared that both Pierce and Charles were desperadoes, that they were contemplating a burglary and that they began the assault upon the policemen. It is interesting to note how the two leading papers of New Orleans, the *Picayune* and the *Times-Democrat*, exert themselves to justify the policemen in the absolutely unprovoked attack upon the two colored men. As these two papers did all in their power to give an excuse for the action of the policemen, it is interesting to note their versions.

The *Times-Democrat* of Tuesday morning, the twenty-fifth, says:

18

Two blacks, who are desperate men, and no doubt will be proven burglars, made it interesting and dangerous for three bluecoats on Dryades street, between Washington Avenue and Sixth Street, the Negroes using pistols first and dropping Patrolman Mora. But the desperate darkies did not go free, for the taller of the two, Robinson, is badly wounded and under cover, while Leonard Pierce is in jail.

For a long time that particular neighborhood has been troubled with bad Negroes, and the neighbors were complaining to the Sixth Precinct police about them. But of late Pierce and Robinson had been camping on a door step on the street, and the people regarded their actions as suspicious. It got to such a point that some of the residents were afraid to go to bed, and last night this was told Sergeant Aucoin, who was rounding up his men. He had just picked up Officers Mora and Cantrell, on Washington Avenue and Dryades Street, and catching a glimpse of the blacks on the steps, he said he would go over and warn the men to get away from the street. So the patrolmen followed, and Sergeant Aucoin asked the smaller fellow, Pierce, if he lived there. The answer was short and impertinent, the black saying he did not, and with that both Pierce and Robinson drew up to their full height.

For the moment the sergeant did not think that the Negroes meant fight, and he was on the point of ordering them away when Robinson slipped his pistol from his pocket. Pierce had his revolver out, too, and he fired twice, point blank at the sergeant, and just then Robinson began shooting at the patrolmen. In a second or so the policemen and blacks were fighting with their revolvers, the sergeant having a duel with Pierce, while Cantrell and Mora drew their line of fire on Robinson, who was working his revolver for all he was worth. One of his shots took Mora in the right hip, another caught his index finger on the right hand, and a third struck the small finger of the left hand. Poor Mora was done for; he could not fight any more, but Cantrell kept up his fire, being answered by the big black. Pierce's revolver broke down, the cartridges snapping, and he threw up his hands, begging for quarter.

The sergeant lowered his pistol and some citizens ran over to where the shooting was going on. One of the bullets that went at Robinson caught him in the breast and he began running, turning out Sixth Street, with Cantrell behind him, shooting every few steps. He was loading his revolver again, but did not use it after the start he took, and in a little while Officer Cantrell lost the man in the darkness.

Pierce was made a prisoner and hurried to the Sixth Precinct police station, where he was charged with shooting and wounding. The sergeant sent for an ambulance, and Mora was taken to the hospital, the wound in the hip being serious.

A search was made for Robinson, but he could not be found, and even at 2 o'clock this morning Captain Day, with Sergeant Aucoin and Corporals Perrier and Trenchard, with a good squad of men, were beating the weeds for the black.

The *New Orleans Picayune* of the same date described the occurrence, and from its account one would think it was an entirely different affair. Both of the two accounts cannot be true, and the unquestioned fact is that neither of them sets out the facts as they occurred. Both accounts attempt to fix the beginning of hostilities upon the colored men, but both were compelled to admit that the colored men were sitting on the doorsteps quietly conversing with one another when the three policemen went up and accosted them. The *Times-Democrat* unguardedly states that one of the two colored men tried to run away; that Mora seized him and then drew his billy and struck him on the head; that Charles broke away from him and started to run, after which the shooting began. The *Picayune*, however, declares that Pierce began the firing and that his two shots point blank at Aucoin were the first shots of the fight. As a matter of fact, Pierce never fired a single shot before he was covered by Aucoin's revolver. Charles and the officers did all the shooting. The *Picayune's* account is as follows:

Patrolman Mora was shot in the right hip and dangerously wounded last night at 11:30 o'clock in Dryades Street, between

20

Washington and Sixth, by two Negroes, who were sitting on a door step in the neighborhood.

The shooting of Patrolman Mora brings to memory the fact that he was one of the partners of Patrolman Trimp, who was shot by a Negro soldier of the United States government during the progress of the Spanish-American war. The shooting of Mora by the Negro last night is a very simple story. At the hour mentioned, three Negro women noticed two suspicious men sitting on a door step in the above locality. The women saw the two men making an apparent inspection of the building. As they told the story, they saw the men look over the fence and examine the window blinds, and they paid particular attention to the make-up of the building, which was a two-story affair. About that time Sergeant J.C. Aucoin and Officers Mora and J.D. Cantrell hove in sight. The women hailed them and described to them the suspicious actions of the two Negroes, who were still sitting on the step. The trio of bluecoats, on hearing the facts, at once crossed the street and accosted the men. The latter answered that they were waiting for a friend whom they were expecting. Not satisfied with this answer, the sergeant asked them where they lived, and they replied "down town," but could not designate the locality. To other questions put by the officers the larger of the two Negroes replied that they had been in town just three days.

As this reply was made, the larger man sprang to his feet, and Patrolman Mora, seeing that he was about to run away, seized him. The Negro took a firm hold on the officer, and a scuffle ensued. Mora, noting that he was not being assisted by his brother officers, drew his billy and struck the Negro on the head. The blow had but little effect upon the man, for he broke away and started down the street. When about ten feet away, the Negro drew his revolver and opened fire on the officer, firing three or four shots. The third shot struck Mora in the right hip, and was subsequently found to have taken an upward course. Although badly wounded, Mora drew his pistol and returned the fire. At his third shot the Negro was noticed to stagger, but he did not fall. He continued his flight. At this moment Sergeant Aucoin seized the other Negro, who proved to be a youth, Leon

21

Pierce. As soon as Officer Mora was shot he sank to the sidewalk, and the other officer ran to the nearest telephone, and sent in a call for the ambulance. Upon its arrival the wounded officer was placed in it and conveyed to the hospital. An examination by the house surgeon revealed the fact that the bullet had taken an upward course. In the opinion of the surgeon the wound was a dangerous one.

But the best proof of the fact that the officers accosted the two colored men and without any warrant or other justification attempted to arrest them, and did actually seize and begin to club one of them, is shown by Officer Mora's own statement. The officer was wounded and had every reason in the world to make his side of the story as good as possible. His statement was made to a *Picayune* reporter and the same was published on the twenty-fifth inst., and is as follows:

I was in the neighborhood of Dryades and Washington Streets, with Sergeant Aucoin and Officer Cantrell, when three Negro women came up and told us that there were two suspicious-looking Negroes sitting on a step on Dryades Street, between Washington and Sixth. We went to the place indicated and found two Negroes. We interrogated them as to who they were, what they were doing and how long they had been here. They replied that they were working for some one and had been in town three days. At about this stage the larger of the two Negroes got up and I grabbed him. The Negro pulled, but I held fast, and he finally pulled me into the street. Here I began using my billet, and the Negro jerked from my grasp and ran. He then pulled a gun and fired. I pulled my gun and returned the fire, each of us firing about three shots. I saw the Negro stumble several times, and I thought I had shot him, but he ran away and I don't know whether any of my shots took effect. Sergeant Aucoin in the meantime held the other man fast. The man was about ten feet from me when he fired, and the three Negresses who told us about the men stood away about twenty-five feet from the shooting.

22

Thus far in the proceeding the Monday night episode results in Officer Mora lying in the station wounded in the hip; Leonard Pierce, one of the colored men, locked up in the station, and Robert Charles, the other colored man, a fugitive, wounded in the leg and sought for by the entire police force of New Orleans. Not sought for, however, to be placed under arrest and given a fair trial and punished if found guilty according to the law of the land, but sought for by a host of enraged, vindictive and fearless officers, who were coolly ordered to kill him on sight. This order is shown by the *Picayune* of the twenty-sixth inst., in which the following statement appears:

In talking to the sergeant about the case, the captain asked about the Negro's fighting ability, and the sergeant answered that Charles, though he called him Robinson then, was a desperate man, and it would be best to shoot him before he was given a chance to draw his pistol upon any of the officers.

This instruction was given before anybody had been killed, and the only evidence that Charles was a desperate man lay in the fact that he had refused to be beaten over the head by Officer Mora for sitting on a step quietly conversing with a friend. Charles resisted an absolutely unlawful attack, and a gun fight followed. Both Mora and Charles were shot, but because Mora was white and Charles was black, Charles was at once declared to be a desperado, made an outlaw, and subsequently a price put upon his head and the mob authorized to shoot him like a dog, on sight.

The New Orleans *Picayune* of Wednesday morning said:

But he has gone, perhaps to the swamps, and the disappointment of the bluecoats in not getting the murderer is expressed in their curses, each man swearing that the signal to halt that will be offered Charles will be a shot.

In that same column of the *Picayune* it was said:

> Hundreds of policemen were about; each corner was guarded by a squad, commanded either by a sergeant or a corporal, and every man had the word to shoot the Negro as soon as he was sighted. He was a desperate black and would be given no chance to take more life.

Legal sanction was given to the mob or any man of the mob to kill Charles at sight by the Mayor of New Orleans, who publicly proclaimed a reward of two hundred and fifty dollars, not for the arrest of Charles, not at all, but the reward was offered for Charles's body, "dead or alive." The advertisement was as follows:

$250 REWARD

Under the authority vested in me by law, I hereby offer, in the name of the city of New Orleans, $250 reward for the capture and delivery, dead or alive, to the authorities of the city, the body of the Negro murderer, ROBERT CHARLES, who, on Tuesday morning, July 24, shot and killed Police Captain JOHN T. DAY and Patrolman PETER J. LAMB, and wounded Patrolman AUGUST T. MORA.

PAUL CAPDEVIELLE,
Mayor

This authority, given by the sergeant to kill Charles on sight, would have been no news to Charles, nor to any colored man in New Orleans, who, for any purpose whatever, even to save his life, raised his hand against a white man. It is now, even as it was in the days of slavery, an unpardonable sin for a Negro to resist a white man, no matter how unjust or unprovoked the white man's attack may be. Charles knew this, and knowing to be captured meant to be killed, he resolved to sell his life as dearly as possible.

The next step in the terrible tragedy occurred between 2:30

and 5 o'clock Tuesday morning, about four hours after the affair on Dryades Street. The man hunt, which had been inaugurated soon after Officer Mora had been carried to the station, succeeded in running down Robert Charles, the wounded fugitive, and located him at 2023 4th Street. It was nearly 2 o'clock in the morning when a large detail of police surrounded the block with the intent to kill Charles on sight. Capt. Day had charge of the squad of police. Charles, the wounded man, was in his house when the police arrived, fully prepared, as results afterward showed, to die in his own home. Capt. Day started for Charles's room. As soon as Charles got sight of him there was a flash, a report, and Day fell dead in his tracks. In another instant Charles was standing in the door, and seeing Patrolman Peter J. Lamb, he drew his gun, and Lamb fell dead. Two other officers, Sergeant Aucoin and Officer Trenchard, who were in the squad, seeing their comrades, Day and Lamb, fall dead, concluded to raise the siege, and both disappeared into an adjoining house, where they blew out their lights so that their cowardly carcasses could be safe from Charles's deadly aim. The calibre of their courage is well shown by the fact that they concluded to save themselves from any harm by remaining prisoners in that dark room until daybreak, out of reach of Charles's deadly rifle. Sergeant Aucoin, who had been so brave a few hours before when seeing the two colored men sitting on the steps, talking together on Dryades Street, and supposing that neither was armed, now showed his true calibre. Now he knew that Charles had a gun and was brave enough to use it, so he hid himself in a room two hours while Charles deliberately walked out of his room and into the street after killing both Lamb and Day. It is also shown, as further evidence of the bravery of some of New Orleans' "finest," that one of them, seeing Capt. Day fall, ran seven blocks before he stopped, afterwards giving the excuse that he was hunting for a patrol box.

At daybreak the officers felt safe to renew the attack upon Charles, so they broke into his room, only to find that—what they probably very well knew—he had gone. It appears that he made his escape by crawling through a hole in the ceiling to a little attic in his house. Here he found that he could not escape except by a window which led into an alley, which had no opening on 4th Street. He scaled the fence and was soon out of reach.

It was now 5 o'clock Tuesday morning, and a general alarm was given. Sergeant Aucoin and Corporal Trenchard, having received a new supply of courage by returning daylight, renewed their effort to capture the man that they had allowed to escape in the darkness. Citizens were called upon to participate in the man hunt and New Orleans was soon the scene of terrible excitement. Officers were present everywhere, and colored men were arrested on all sides upon the pretext that they were impertinent and "game niggers." An instance is mentioned in the *Times-Democrat* of the twenty-fifth and shows the treatment which unoffending colored men received at the hands of some of the officers. This instance shows Corporal Trenchard, who displayed such remarkable bravery on Monday night in dodging Charles's revolver, in his true light. It shows how brave a white man is when he has a gun attacking a Negro who is a helpless prisoner. The account is as follows:

The police made some arrests in the neighborhood of the killing of the two officers. Mobs of young darkies gathered everywhere. These Negroes talked and joked about the affair, and many of them were for starting a race war on the spot. It was not until several of these little gangs amalgamated and started demonstrations that the police commenced to act. Nearly a dozen arrests were made within an hour, and everybody in the vicinity was in a tremor of excitement. It was about 1 o'clock that the Negroes on Fourth Street became very noisy, and George Meyers, who lives on Sixth Street, near Rampart, appeared to be one of the prime movers in a little riot that was rapidly developing. Policeman Exnicios and Sheridan placed him under arrest, and owing to the fact that the patrol wagon had just left with a number of prisoners, they walked him toward St. Charles Avenue in order to get a conveyance to take him to the Sixth Precinct station. A huge crowd of Negroes followed the officers and their prisoners. Between Dryades and Baronne, on Sixth, Corporal Trenchard met the trio. He had his pistol in his hand and he came on them running. The Negroes in the wake of the officers, and prisoner took to flight immediately. Some disappeared through gates and some over fences and into yards, for Trenchard, visibly excited, was waving his revolver in the air and was threatening to shoot. He joined the officers in their walk toward St. Charles Street, and the way he acted led the white people who were witnessing the affair to believe that his prisoner was the wanted Negro. At every step he would punch him or hit him with the barrel of his pistol, and the onlookers cried, "Lynch him!" "Kill him!" and other expressions until the spectators were thoroughly wrought up. At St. Charles Street Trenchard desisted, and, calling an empty ice wagon, threw the Negro into the body of the vehicle and ordered Officer Exnicios to take him to the Sixth Precinct station.

The ride to the station was a wild one. Exnicios had all he could do to watch his prisoner. A gang climbed into the wagon and administered a terrible thrashing to the black en route. It took a half hour to reach the police station, for the mule that was drawing the wagon was not overly fast. When the station was reached a mob of nearly 200 howling white youths was awaiting it. The noise they made was something terrible. Meyers was howling for mercy before he reached the ground. The mob dragged him from the wagon, the officer with him. Then began a torrent of abuse for the unfortunate prisoner.

The station door was but thirty feet away, but it took Exnicios nearly five minutes to fight his way through the mob to the door. There were no other officers present, and the station seemed to be deserted. Neither the doorman nor the clerk paid any attention to the noise on the outside. As the result, the maddened crowd wrought their vengeance on the Negro. He was punched, kicked, bruised and torn. The clothes were ripped from his back, while his face after that few minutes was unrecognizable.

This was the treatment accorded and permitted to a helpless prisoner because he was black. All day Wednesday the man hunt continued. The excitement caused by the deaths of Day and Lamb became intense. The officers of the law knew they were trailing a man whose aim was deadly and whose courage they had never seen surpassed. Commenting upon the marksmanship of the man which the paper styled a fiend, the *Times-Democrat* of Wednesday said:

> One of the extraordinary features of the tragedy was the marksmanship displayed by the Negro desperado. His aim was deadly and his coolness must have been something phenomenal. The two shots that killed Captain Day and Patrolman Lamb struck their victims in the head, a circumstance remarkable enough in itself, considering the suddenness and fury of the onslaught and the darkness that reigned in the alley way.
>
> Later on Charles fired at Corporal Perrier, who was standing at least seventy-five yards away. The murderer appeared at the gate, took lightning aim along the side of the house, and sent a bullet whizzing past the officer's ear. It was a close shave, and a few inches' deflection would no doubt have added a fourth victim to the list.
>
> At the time of the affray there is good reason to believe that Charles was seriously wounded, and at any event he had lost quantities of blood. His situation was as critical as it is possible to imagine, yet he shot like an expert in a target range. The circumstance shows the desperate character of the fiend, and his terrible dexterity with weapons makes him one of the most formidable monsters that has ever been loose upon the community.

Wednesday New Orleans was in the hands of a mob. Charles, still sought for and still defending himself, had killed four policemen, and everybody knew that he intended to die fighting. Unable to vent its vindictiveness and bloodthirsty vengeance upon Charles, the mob turned its attention to other colored men who happened to get in the path of its fury. Even colored women, as has happened many times before, were assaulted and beaten and killed by the brutal hoodlums who thronged the streets. The reign of absolute lawlessness began about 8 o'clock Wednesday night. The mob gathered near the Lee statue and was soon making its way to the place where the officers had been shot by Charles. Describing the mob, the *Times-Democrat* of Thursday morning says:

The gathering in the square, which numbered about 700, eventually became in a measure quiet, and a large, lean individual, in poor attire and with unshaven face, leaped upon a box that had been brought for the purpose, and in a voice that under no circumstances could be heard at a very great distance, shouted: "Gentlemen, I am the Mayor of Kenner." He did not get a chance for some minutes to further declare himself, for the voice of the rabble swung over his like a huge wave over a sinking craft. He stood there, however, wildly waving his arms and demanded a hearing, which was given him when the uneasiness of the mob was quieted for a moment or so.

"I am from Kenner, gentlemen, and I have come down to New Orleans tonight to assist you in teaching the blacks a lesson. I have killed a Negro before, and in revenge of the wrong wrought upon you and yours, I am willing to kill again. The only way that you can teach these Niggers a lesson and put them in their place is to go out and lynch a few of them as an object lesson. String up a few of them, and the others will trouble you no more. That is the only thing to do—kill them, string them up, lynch them! I will lead you, if you will but follow. On to the Parish Prison and lynch Pierce!"

They bore down on the Parish Prison like an avalanche, but the avalanche split harmlessly on the blank walls of the jail, and Remy Klock sent out a brief message: "You can't have Pierce, and you can't get in." Up to that time the mob had had no opposition, but Klock's answer chilled them considerably. There was no deep-seated desperation in the crowd after all, only, that wild lawlessness which leads to deeds of cruelty, but not to stubborn battle. Around the corner from the prison is a row of pawn and second-hand shops,

29

and to these the mob took like the ducks to the proverbial mill-pond, and the devastation they wrought upon Mr. Fink's establishment was beautiful in its line.

Everything from breast pins to horse pistols went into the pockets of the crowd, and in the melee a man was shot down, while just around the corner somebody planted a long knife in the body of a little newsboy for no reason as yet shown. Every now and then a Negro would be flushed somewhere in the outskirts of the crowd and left beaten to a pulp. Just how many were roughly handled will never be known, but the unlucky thirteen had been severely beaten and maltreated up to a late hour, a number of those being in the Charity Hospital under the bandages and courtplaster of the doctors.

The first colored man to meet death at the hands of the mob was a passenger on a street car. The mob had broken itself into fragments after its disappointment at the jail, each fragment looking for a Negro to kill. The bloodthirsty cruelty of one crowd is thus described by the *Times-Democrat*:

"We will get a Nigger down here, you bet!" was the yelling boast that went up from a thousand throats, and for the first time the march of the mob was directed toward the downtown sections. The words of the rioters were prophetic, for just as Canal Street was reached a car on the Villere line came along.

"Stop that car!" cried half a hundred men. The advance guard, heeding the injunction, rushed up to the slowly moving car, and several, seizing the trolley, jerked it down.

"Here's a Nigro!" said half a dozen men who sprang upon the car.

The car was full of passengers at the time, among them several women. When the trolley was pulled down and the car thrown in total darkness, the latter began to scream, and for a moment or so it looked as if the life of every person in the car was in peril, for some of the crowd with demoniacal yells of "There he goes!" began to fire their weapons indiscriminately.

The passengers in the car hastily jumped to the ground and joined the crowd, as it was evidently the safest place to be.

"Where's that Nigger?" was the query passed along the line, and with that the search began in earnest. The Negro, after jumping off the car, lost himself for a few moments in the crowd, but after a brief search he was again located. The slight delay seemed, if possible, only to whet the desire of the bloodthirsty crowd, for the reappearance of the Negro was the signal for a chorus of screams and pistol shots directed at the fugitive. With the speed of a deer, the man ran straight from the corner of Canal and Villere to Customhouse Street. The pursuers, closely following, kept up a running fire, but notwithstanding the fact that they were right at the Negro's heels their aim was poor and their bullets went wide of the mark.

The Negro, on reaching Customhouse Street, darted from the sidewalk out into the middle of the street. This was the worst maneuver that he could have made, as it brought him directly under the light from an arc lamp, located on a nearby corner. When the Negro came plainly in view of the foremost of the closely following mob they directed a volley at him. Half a dozen pistols flashed simultaneously, and one of the bullets evidently found its mark, for the Negro stopped short, threw up his hands, wavered for a moment, and then started to run again. This stop, slight as it was, proved fatal to the Negro's chances, for he had not gotten twenty steps farther when several of the men in advance of the others reached his side. A burly fellow, grabbing him with one hand, dealt him a terrible blow on the head with the other. The wounded man sank to the ground. The crowd pressed around him and began to beat him and stamp him. The men in the rear pressed forward and those beating the man were shoved forward. The half-dead Negro, when he was freed from his assailants, crawled over to the gutter. The men behind, however, stopped pushing when those in front yelled, "We've got him," and then it was that the attack on the bleeding Negro was resumed. A vicious kick directed at the Negro's head sent him into the gutter, and for a moment the body sank from view beneath the muddy, slimy water. "Pull him out; don't let him drown," was the cry, and instantly several of the men around the half-drowned Negro bent down and

31

drew the body out. Twisting the body around they drew the head and shoulders up on the street, while from the waist down the Negro's body remained under the water. As soon as the crowd saw that the Negro was still alive they again began to beat and kick him. Every few moments they would stop and striking matches look into the man's face to see if he still lived. To better see if he was dead they would stick lighted matches to his eyes. Finally, believing he was dead they left him and started out to look for other Negroes. Just about this time some one yelled, "He ain't dead," and the men came back and renewed the attack. While the men were beating and pounding the prostrate form with stones and sticks a man in the crowd ran up, and crying, "I'll fix the d—- Negro," poked the muzzle of a pistol almost against the body and fired. This shot must have ended the man's life, for he lay like a stone, and realizing that they were wasting energy in further attacks, the men left their victim lying in the street.

The same paper, on the same day, July 26, describes the brutal butchery of an aged colored man early in the morning:

Baptiste Philo, a Negro, seventy-five years of age, was a victim of mob violence at Kerlerec and North Peters Streets about 2:30 o'clock this morning. The old man is employed about the French Market, and was on his way there when he was met by a crowd and desperately shot. The old man found his way to the Third Precinct police station, where it was found that he had received a ghastly wound in the abdomen. The ambulance was summoned and he was conveyed to the Charity Hospital. The students pronounced the wound fatal after a superficial examination.

Mob rule continued Thursday, its violence increasing every hour, until 2 p.m., when the climax seemed to be reached. The fact that colored men and women had been made the victims of brutal mobs, chased through the streets, killed upon the highways and butchered in their homes, did not call the best element in New Orleans to active exertion in behalf of law and order. The killing of a few Negroes more or less by irresponsible mobs does not cut much figure in Louisiana. But when the reign of mob law exerts a depressing influence upon the stock market and city securities begin to show unsteady standing in money centers, then the strong arm of the good white people of the South asserts itself and order is quickly brought out of chaos. It was so with New Orleans on that Thursday. The better element of the white citizens began to realize that New Orleans in the hands of a mob would not prove a promising investment for Eastern capital, so the better element began to stir itself, not for the purpose of punishing the brutality against the Negroes who had been beaten, or bringing to justice the murderers of those who had been killed, but for the purpose of saving the city's credit. The *Times-Democrat*, upon this phase of the situation on Friday morning says:

When it became known later in the day that State bonds had depreciated from a point to a point and a half on the New York market a new phase of seriousness was manifest to the business community. Thinking men realized that a continuance of unchecked disorder would strike a body blow to the credit of the city and in all probability would complicate the negotiation of the forthcoming improvement bonds. The bare thought that such a disaster might be brought about by a few irresponsible boys, tramps and ruffians, inflamed popular indignation to fever pitch. It was all that was needed to bring to the aid of the authorities the active personal cooperation of the entire better element.

With the financial credit of the city at stake, the good citizens rushed to the rescue, and soon the Mayor was able to mobilize a posse of 1,000 willing men to assist the police in maintaining order, but rioting still continued in different sections of the city. Colored men and women were beaten, chased and shot whenever they made their appearance upon the street. Late in the night a most despicable piece of villainy occurred on Rousseau Street, where an aged colored woman was killed by the mob. The *Times-Democrat* thus describes, the murder:

> Hannah Mabry, an old Negress, was shot and desperately wounded shortly after midnight this morning while sleeping in her home at No. 1929 Rousseau Street. It was the work of a mob, and was evidently well planned so far as escape was concerned, for the place was reached by police officers, and a squad of the volunteer police within a very short time after the reports of the shots, but not a prisoner was secured. The square was surrounded, but the mob had scattered in several directions, and, the darkness of the neighborhood aiding them, not one was taken.
>
> At the time the mob made the attack on the little house there were also in it David Mabry, the sixty-two-year-old husband of the wounded woman; her son, Harry Mabry; his wife, Fannie, and an infant child. The young couple with their babe could not be found after the whole affair was over, and they either escaped or were hustled off by the mob. A careful search of the whole neighborhood was made, but no trace of them could be found.
>
> The little place occupied by the Mabry family is an old cottage on the swamp side of Rousseau Street. It is furnished with slat shutters to both doors and windows. These shutters had been pulled off by the mob and the volleys fired through the glass doors. The younger Mabrys, father, mother and child, were asleep in the first room at the time. Hannah Mabry and her old husband were sleeping in the next room. The old couple occupied the same bed, and it is miraculous that the old man did not share the fate of his spouse.
>
> Officer Bitterwolf, who was one of the first on the scene, said that he was about a block and a half away with Officers Fordyce and Sweeney. There were about twenty shots fired, and the trio raced to the cottage. They saw twenty or thirty men running down Rousseau Street. Chase was given and the crowd turned toward the river and scattered into several vacant lots in the neighborhood.
>
> The volunteer police stationed at the Sixth Precinct had about five blocks to run before they arrived. They also moved on the reports of

the firing, and in a remarkably short time the square was surrounded, but no one could be taken. As they ran to the scene they were assailed on every hand with vile epithets and the accusation of "Nigger lovers."

Rousseau Street, where the cottage is situated, is a particularly dark spot, and no doubt the members of the mob were well acquainted with the neighborhood, for the officers said that they seemed to sink into the earth, so completely and quickly did they disappear after they had completed their work, which was complete with the firing of the volley.

Hannah Mabry was taken to the Charity Hospital in the ambulance, where it was found on examination that she had been shot through the right lung, and that the wound was a particularly serious one.

Her old husband was found in the little wrecked home well nigh distracted with fear and grief. It was he who informed the police that at the time of the assault the younger Mabrys occupied the front room. As he ran about the little home as well as his feeble condition would permit he severely lacerated his feet on the glass broken from the windows and door. He was escorted to the Sixth Precinct station, where he was properly cared for. He could not realize why his little family had been so murderously attacked, and was inconsolable when his wife was driven off in the ambulance piteously moaning in her pain.

The search for the perpetrators of the outrage was thorough, but both police and armed force of citizens had only their own efforts to rely on. The residents of the neighborhood were aroused by the firing, but they would give no help in the search and did not appear in the least concerned over the affair. Groups were on almost every doorstep, and some of them even jeered in a quiet way at the men who were voluntarily attempting to capture the members of the mob. Absolutely no information could be had from any of them, and the whole affair had the appearance of being the work of roughs who either lived in the vicinity, or their friends.

DEATH OF CHARLES

Friday witnessed the final act in the bloody drama begun by the three police officers, Aucoin, Mora and Cantrelle. Betrayed into the hands of the police, Charles, who had already sent two of his would-be murderers to their death, made a last stand in a small building, 1210 Saratoga Street, and, still defying his pursuers, fought a mob of twenty thousand people, single-handed and alone, killing three more men, mortally wounding two more and seriously wounding nine others. Unable to get to him in his stronghold, the besiegers set fire to his house of refuge. While the building was burning Charles was shooting, and every crack of his death-dealing rifle added another victim to the price which he had placed upon his own life. Finally, when fire and smoke became too much for flesh and blood to stand, the long sought for fugitive appeared in the door, rifle in hand, to charge the countless guns that were drawn upon him. With a courage which was indescribable, he raised his gun to fire again, but this time it failed, for a hundred shots riddled his body, and he fell dead face fronting to the mob. This last scene in the terrible drama is thus described in the *Times-Democrat* of July 26:

Early yesterday afternoon, at 3 o'clock or thereabouts, Police Sergeant Gabriel Porteus was instructed by Chief Gaster to go to a house at No. 1210 Saratoga Street, and search it for the fugitive murderer, Robert Charles. A private "tip" had been received at the headquarters that the fiend was hiding somewhere on the premises.

Sergeant Porteus took with him Corporal John R. Lally and Officers Zeigel and Essey. The house to which they were directed is a small, double frame cottage, standing flush with Saratoga Street, near the corner of Clio. It has two street entrances and two rooms on each side, one in front and one in the rear. It belongs to the type of cheap little dwellings commonly tenanted by Negroes.

Sergeant Porteus left Ziegel and Essey to guard the outside and went with Corporal Lally to the rear house, where he found Jackson and his wife in the large room on the left. What immediately ensued is only known by the Negroes. They say the sergeant began to question them about their lodgers and finally asked them whether they knew anything about Robert Charles. They strenuously denied all knowledge of his whereabouts.

The Negroes lied. At that very moment the hunted and desperate murderer lay concealed not a dozen feet away. Near the rear, left-hand corner of the room is a closet or pantry, about three feet deep, and perhaps eight feet long. The door was open and Charles was crouching, Winchester in hand, in the dark further end.

Near the closet door was a bucket of water, and Jackson says that Sergeant Porteous walked toward it to get a drink. At the next moment a shot rang out and the brave officer fell dead. Lally was shot directly afterward. Exactly how and where will never be known, but the probabilities are that the black fiend sent a bullet into him before he recovered from his surprise at the sudden onslaught. Then the murderer dashed out of the back door and disappeared.

The neighborhood was already agog with the tragic events of the two preceding days, and the sound of the shots was a signal for wild and instant excitement. In a few moments a crowd had gathered and people were pouring in by the hundred from every point of the compass. Jackson and his wife had fled and at first nobody knew what had happened, but the surmise that Charles had recommended his bloody work was on every tongue and soon some of the bolder found their way to the house in the rear. There the bleeding forms of the two policemen told the story.

Lally was still breathing, and a priest was sent for to administer the last rites. Father Fitzgerald responded, and while he was bending over the dying man the outside throng was rushing wildly through the surrounding yards and passageways searching for the murderer.

"Where is he?" "What has become of him?" were the questions on every lip.

Suddenly the answer came in a shot from the room directly overhead. It was fired through a window facing Saratoga Street, and the bullet struck down a young man named Alfred J. Bloomfield, who was standing in the narrow passage-way between the two houses. He fell on his knees and a second bullet stretched him dead.

When he fled from the closet Charles took refuge in the upper story of the house. There are four windows on that floor, two facing toward Saratoga Street and two toward Rampart. The murderer kicked several breaches in the frail central partition, so he could rush from side to side, and like a trapped beast, prepared to make his last stand.

Nobody had dreamed that he was still in the house, and when Bloomfield was shot there was a headlong stampede. It was some minutes before the exact situation was understood. Then rifles and pistols began to speak, and a hail of bullets poured against the blind frontage of the old house. Every one hunted some coign of vantage, and many climbed to adjacent roofs. Soon the glass of the four upper windows was shattered by flying lead. The fusillade sounded like a battle, and the excitement upon the streets was indescribable.

Throughout all this hideous uproar Charles seems to have retained a certain diabolical coolness. He kept himself mostly out of sight, but now and then he thrust the gleaming barrel of his rifle through one of the shattered window panes and fired at his besiegers. He worked the weapon with incredible rapidity, discharging from three to five cartridges each time before leaping back to a place of safety. These replies came from all four windows indiscriminately, and showed that he was keeping a close watch in every direction. His wonderful marksmanship never failed him for a moment, and when he missed it was always by the narrowest margin only.

On the Rampart Street side of the house there are several sheds, commanding an excellent range of the upper story. Detective Littleton, Andrew Van Kuren of the Workhouse force and several others climbed upon one of these and opened fire on the upper windows, shooting whenever they could catch a glimpse of the assassin. Charles responded with his rifle, and presently Van Kuren climbed down to find a better position. He was crossing the end of the shed when he was killed.

Another of Charles's bullets found its billet in the body of Frank Evans, an ex-member of the police force. He was on the Rampart Street side firing whenever he had an opportunity. Officer J.W. Bofill and A.S. Leclerc were also wounded in the fusillade.

While the events thus briefly outlined were transpiring time was a-wing, and the cooler headed in the crowd began to realize that some quick and desperate expedient must be adopted to insure the capture of the fiend and to avert what might be a still greater tragedy than any yet enacted. For nearly two hours the desperate monster had held his besiegers at bay, darkness would soon be at hand and no one could predict what might occur if he made a dash for liberty in the dark.

At this critical juncture it was suggested that the house be fired. The plan came as an inspiration, and was adopted as the only solution of the situation. The wretched old rookery counted for nothing against the possible continued sacrifice of human life, and steps were immediately taken to apply the torch. The fire department had been summoned to the scene soon after the shooting began; its officers were warned to be ready to prevent a spread of the conflagration, and several men rushed into the lower right-hand room and started a blaze in one corner.

They first fired an old mattress, and soon smoke was pouring out in dense volumes. It filled the interior of the ramshackle structure, and it was evident that the upper story would soon become untenable. An interval of tense excitement followed, and all eyes were strained for a glimpse of the murderer when he emerged.

Then came the thrilling climax. Smoked out of his den, the desperate fiend descended the stairs and entered the lower room. Some say he dashed into the yard, glaring around vainly for some avenue of escape; but, however that may be, he was soon a few moments later moving about behind the lower windows. A dozen shots were sent through the wall in the hope of reaching him, but he escaped unscathed. Then suddenly the door on the right was flung open and he dashed out. With head lowered and rifle raised ready to fire on the instant, Charles dashed straight for the rear door of the front cottage. To reach it he had to traverse a little walk shaded by a vineclad arbor. In the back room, with a cocked revolver in his hand, was Dr. C.A. Noiret, a young medical student, who was aiding the citizens' posse. As he sprang through the door Charles fired a shot, and the bullet whizzed past the doctor's head. Before it could be repeated Noiret's pistol cracked and the murderer reeled, turned half around and fell on his back. The doctor sent another ball into his body as he struck the floor, and half a dozen men, swarming into the room from the front, riddled the corpse with bullets.

Private Adolph Anderson of the Connell Rifles was the first man to announce the death of the wretch. He rushed to the street door, shouted the news to the crowd, and a moment later the bleeding body was dragged to the pavement and made the target of a score of pistols. It was shot, kicked and beaten almost out of semblance to humanity....

The limp dead body was dropped at the edge of the sidewalk and from there dragged to the muddy roadway by half a hundred hands. There in the road more shots were fired into the body. Corporal Trenchard, a brother-in-law of Porteus, led the shooting into the inanimate clay. With each shot there was a cheer for the work that had been done and curses and imprecations on the inanimate mass of riddled flesh that was once Robert Charles.

Cries of "Burn him! Burn him!" were heard from Clio Street all the way to Erato Street, and it was with difficulty that the crowd was restrained from totally destroying the wretched dead body. Some of those who agitated burning even secured a large vessel of kerosene, which had previously been brought to the scene for the purpose of firing Charles's refuge, and for a time it looked as though this vengeance might be wreaked on the body. The officers, however, restrained this move, although they were powerless to prevent the stamping and kicking of the body by the enraged crowd.

After the infuriated citizens had vented their spleen on the body of the dead Negro it was loaded into the patrol wagon. The police raised the body of the heavy black from the ground and literally chucked it into the space on the floor of the wagon between the seats. They threw it with a curse hissed more than uttered and born of the bitterness which was rankling in their breasts at the thought of Charles having taken so wantonly the lives of four of the best of their fellow-officers.

When the murderer's body landed in the wagon it fell in such a position that the hideously mutilated head, kicked, stamped and crushed, hung over the end.

As the wagon moved off, the followers, who were protesting against its being carried off, declaring that it should be burned, poked and struck it with sticks, beating it into such a condition that it was utterly impossible to tell what the man ever looked like.

As the patrol wagon rushed through the rough street, jerking and swaying from one side of the thoroughfare to the other, the gory, mud-smeared head swayed and swung and jerked about in a sickening manner, the dark blood dripping on the steps and spattering the body of the wagon and the trousers of the policemen standing on the step.

MOB BRUTALITY

The brutality of the mob was further shown by the unspeakable cruelty with which it beat, shot and stabbed to death an unoffending colored man, name unknown, who happened to be walking on the street with no thought that he would be set upon and killed simply because he was a colored man. The *Times-Democrat*'s description of the outrage is as follows:

> While the fight between the Negro desperado and the citizens was in progress yesterday afternoon at Clio and Saratoga Streets another tragedy was being enacted downtown in the French quarter, but it was a very one-sided affair. The object of the white man's wrath was, of course, a Negro, but, unlike Charles, he showed no fight, but tried to escape from the furious mob which was pursuing him, and which finally put an end to his existence in a most cruel manner.
>
> The Negro, whom no one seemed to know—at any rate no one could be found in the vicinity of the killing who could tell who he was—was walking along the levee, as near as could be learned, when he was attacked by a number of white longshoremen or screwmen. For what reason, if there was any reason other than the fact that he was a Negro, could not be learned, and immediately they pounced upon him he broke ground and started on a desperate run for his life.
>
> The hunted Negro started off the levee toward the French Vegetable Market, changed his course out the sidewalk toward Gallatin Street. The angry, yelling mob was close at his heels, and increasing steadily as each block was traversed. At Gallatin Street he turned up that thoroughfare, doubled back into North Peters Street and ran into the rear of No. 1216 of that street, which is occupied by Chris Reuter as a commission store and residence.
>
> He rushed frantically through the place and out on to the gallery

on the Gallatin Street side. From this gallery he jumped to the street and fell flat on his back on the sidewalk. Springing to his feet as soon as possible, with a leaden, hail fired by the angry mob whistling about him, he turned to his merciless pursuers in an appealing way, and, throwing up one hand, told them not to shoot any more, that they could take him as he was.

But the hail of lead continued, and the unfortunate Negro finally dropped to the sidewalk, mortally wounded. The mob then rushed upon him, still continuing the fusillade, and upon reaching his body a number of Italians, who had joined the howling mob, reached down and stabbed him in the back and buttock with big knives. Others fired shots into his head until his teeth were shot out, three shots having been fired into his mouth. There were bullet wounds all over his body.

Others who witnessed the affair declared that the man was fired at as he was running up the stairs leading to the living apartments above the store, and that after jumping to the sidewalk and being knocked down by a bullet he jumped up and ran across the street, then ran back and tried to get back into the commission store. The Italians, it is said, were all drunk, and had been shooting firecrackers. Tiring of this, they began shooting at Negroes, and when the unfortunate man who was killed ran by they joined in the chase.

No one was arrested for the shooting, the neighborhood having been deserted by the police, who were sent up to the place where Charles was fighting so desperately. No one could or would give the names of any of those who had participated in the chase and the killing, nor could any one be found who knew who the Negro was. The patrol wagon was called and the terribly mutilated body sent to the morgue and the coroner notified.

The murdered Negro was copper colored, about 5 feet 11 inches in height, about 35 years of age, and was dressed in blue overalls and a brown slouch hat. At 10:30 o'clock the vicinity of the French Market was very quiet. Squads of special officers were patrolling the neighborhood, and there did not seem to be any prospects of disorder.

During the entire time the mob held the city in its hands and went about holding up street cars and searching them, taking from them colored men to assault, shoot and kill, chasing colored men upon the public square, through alleys and into houses of anybody who would take them in, breaking into the homes of defenseless colored men and women and beating aged and decrepit men and women to death, the police and the legally constituted authorities showed plainly where their sympathies were, for in no case reported through the daily papers does there appear the arrest, trial and conviction of one of the mob for any of the brutalities which occurred. The ringleaders of the mob were at no time disguised. Men were chased, beaten and killed by white brutes, who boasted of their crimes, and the murderers still walk the streets of New Orleans, well known and absolutely exempt from prosecution. Not only were they exempt from prosecution by the police while the town was in the hands of the mob, but even now that law and order is supposed to resume control, these men, well known, are not now, nor ever will be, called to account for the unspeakable brutalities of that terrible week. On the other hand, the colored men who were beaten by the police and dragged into the station for purposes of intimidation, were quickly called up before the courts and fined or sent to jail upon the statement of the police. Instances of Louisiana justice as it is dispensed in New Orleans are here quoted from the *Times-Democrat* of July 26:

JUSTICE DEALT OUT TO FOLK WHO TALKED TOO MUCH

All the Negroes and whites who were arrested in the vicinity of Tuesday's tragedy had a hard time before Recorder Hughes yesterday. Lee Jackson was the first prisoner, and the evidence established that he made his way to the vicinity of the crime and told his Negro friends that he thought a good many more policemen ought to be killed. Jackson said he was drunk when he made the remark. He was fined $25 or thirty days.

John Kennedy was found wandering about the street Tuesday

night with an open razor in his hand, and he was given $25 or thirty days.

Edward McCarthy, a white man, who arrived only four days since from New York, went to the scene of the excitement at the corner of Third and Rampart Streets, and told the Negroes that they were as good as any white man. This remark was made by McCarthy, as another white man said the Negroes should be lynched. McCarthy told the recorder that he considered a Negro as good as a white in body and soul. He was fined $25 or thirty days.

James Martin, Simon Montegut, Eddie McCall, Alex Washington and Henry Turner were up for failing to move on. Martin proved that he was at the scene to assist the police and was discharged. Montegut, being a cripple, was also released, but the others were fined $25 or thirty days each.

Eddie Williams for refusing to move on was given $25 or thirty days.

Matilda Gamble was arrested by the police for saying that two officers were killed and it was a pity more were not shot. She was given $25 or thirty days.

INSOLENT BLACKS

"Recorder Hughes received Negroes in the first recorder's office yesterday morning in a way that they will remember for a long time, and all of them were before the magistrate for having caused trouble through incendiary remarks concerning the death of Captain Day and Patrolman Lamb."

"Lee Jackson was before the recorder and was fined $25 or thirty days. He was lippy around where the trouble happened Tuesday morning, and some white men punched him good and hard and the police took him. Then the recorder gave him a dose, and now he is in the parish prison."

"John Kennedy was another black who got into trouble. He said that the shooting of the police by Charles was a good thing, and for this he was pounded. Patrolman Lorenzo got him and saved him from being lynched, for the black had an open razor. He was fined $25 or thirty days."

"Edward McCarthy, a white man, mixed up with the crowd, and an expression of sympathy nearly cost him his head, for some whites about started for him, administering licks and blows with fists and umbrellas. The recorder fined him $25 or thirty days. He is from New York."

"Then James Martin, a white man, and Simon Montegut, Eddie Call, Henry Turner and Alex Washington were before the magistrate for having failed to move on when the police ordered them from the square where the bluecoats were Tuesday, waiting in the hope of catching Charles. All save Martin and Montegut were fined."

"Eddie Williams, a little Negro who was extremely fresh with the police, was fined $10 or ten days."

SHOCKING BRUTALITY

The whole city was at the mercy of the mob and the display of brutality was a disgrace to civilization. One instance is described in the *Picayune* as follows:

A smaller party detached itself from the mob at Washington and Rampart Streets, and started down the latter thoroughfare. One of the foremost spied a Negro, and immediately there was a rush for the unfortunate black man. With the sticks they had torn from fences on the line of march the young outlaws attacked the black and clubbed him unmercifully, acting more like demons than human beings. After being severely beaten over the head, the Negro started to run with the whole gang at his heels. Several revolvers were brought into play and pumped their lead at the refugee. The Negro made rapid progress and took refuge behind the blinds of a little cottage in Rampart Street, but he had been seen, and the mob hauled him from his hiding place and again commenced beating him. There were more this time, some twenty or thirty, all armed with sticks and heavy clubs, and under their incessant blows the Negro could not last long. He begged for mercy, and his cries were most pitiful, but a mob has no heart, and his cries were only answered with more blows.

"For God's sake, boss, I ain't done nothin'. Don't kill me. I swear I ain't done nothin'."

The white brutes turned

A Deaf Ear to the Pitying Cries

of the black wretch and the drubbing continued. The cries subsided into moans, and soon the black swooned away into unconsciousness. Still not content with their heartless work, they pulled the Negro out

47

and kicked him into the gutter. For the time those who had beaten the black seemed satisfied and left him groaning in the gutter, but others came up, and, regretting that they had not had a hand in the affair, they determined to evidence their bravery to their fellows and beat the man while he was in the gutter, hurling rocks and stones at his black form. One thoughtless white brute, worse even than the black slayer of the police officers, thought to make himself a hero in the eyes of his fellows and fired his revolver repeatedly into the helpless wretch. It was dark and the fellow probably aimed carelessly. After firing three or four shots he also left without knowing what extent of injury he inflicted on the black wretch who was left lying in the gutter.

MURDER ON THE LEVEE

One part of the crowd made a raid on the tenderloin district, hoping to find there some belated Negro for a sacrifice. They were urged on by the white prostitutes, who applauded their murderous mission. Says an account:

> The red light district was all excitement. Women—that is, the white women—were out on their stoops and peeping over their galleries and through their windows and doors, shouting to the crowd to go on with their work, and kill Negroes for them.
>
> "Our best wishes, boys," they encouraged; and the mob answered with shouts, and whenever a Negro house was sighted a bombardment was started on the doors and windows.

No colored men were found on the streets until the mob reached Custom House Place and Villiers Streets. Here a victim was found and brutally put to death. The *Picayune* description is as follows:

> Some stragglers had run a Negro into a car at the corner of Bienville and Villere Streets. He was seeking refuge in the conveyance, and he believed that the car would not be stopped and could speed along. But the mob determined to stop the car, and ordered the motorman to halt. He put on his brake. Some white men were in the car.
>
> "Get out, fellows," shouted several of the mob.
>
> "All whites fall out," was the second cry, and the poor Negro understood that it was meant that he should stay in the car.
>
> He wanted to save his life. The poor fellow crawled under the seats. But some one in the crowd saw him and yelled that he was hiding. Two or three men climbed through the windows with their pistols;

others jumped over the motorman's board, and dozens tumbled into the rear of the car. Big, strong hands got the Negro by the shirt. He was dragged out of the conveyance, and was pushed to the street. Some fellow ran up and struck him with a club. The blow was heavy, but it did not fell him, and the Negro ran toward Canal Street, stealing along the wall of the Tulane Medical Building. Fifty men ran after him, caught the poor fellow and hurried him back into the crowd. Fists were aimed at him, then clubs went upon his shoulders, and finally the black plunged into the gutter.

A gun was fired, and the Negro, who had just gotten to his feet, dropped again. He tried to get up, but a volley was sent after him, and in a little while he was dead.

The crowd looked on at the terrible work. Then the lights in the houses of ill-fame began to light up again, and women peeped out of the blinds. The motorman was given the order to go on. The gong clanged and the conveyance sped out of the way. For half an hour the crowd held their place at the corner, then the patrol wagon came and the body was picked up and hurried to the morgue.

Coroner Richard held an autopsy on the body of the Negro who was forced out of car 98 of the Villere line and shot down. It was found that he was wounded four times, the most serious wound being that which struck him in the right side, passing through the lungs, and causing hemorrhages, which brought about death.

Nobody tried to identify the poor fellow and his name is unknown.

A VICTIM IN THE MARKET

Soon after the murder of the man on the street car many of the same mob marched down to the market place. There they found a colored market man named Louis Taylor, who had gone to begin his early morning's work. He was at once set upon by the mob and killed. The *Picayune* account says:

Between 1 and 2 o'clock this morning a mob of several hundred men and boys, made up of participants in many of the earlier affairs, marched on the French Market. Louis Taylor, a Negro vegetable carrier, who is about thirty years of age, was sitting at the soda water stand. As soon as the mob saw him fire was opened and the Negro took to his heels. He ran directly into another section of the mob and any number of shots were fired at him. He fell, face down, on the floor of the market.

The police in the neighborhood rallied hurriedly and found the victim of mob violence seemingly lifeless. Before they arrived the Negro had been beaten severely about the head and body. The ambulance was summoned and Taylor was carried to the charity hospital, where it was found that he had been shot through the abdomen and arm. The examination was a hurried one, but it sufficed to show that Taylor was mortally wounded.

After shooting Taylor the members of the mob were pluming themselves on their exploit. "The Nigger was at the soda water stand and we commenced shooting him," said one of the rioters. "He put his hands up and ran, and we shot until he fell. I understand that he is still alive. If he is, he is a wonder. He was certainly shot enough to be killed."

The members of the mob readily admitted that they had taken part in the assaults which marked the earlier part of the evening.

"We were up on Jackson Avenue and killed a Nigger on Villere Street. We came down here, saw a nigger and killed him, too." This was the way they told the story.

"Boys, we are out of ammunition," said someone.

"Well, we will keep on like we are, and if we can't get some before morning, we will take it. We have got to keep this thing up, now we have started."

This declaration was greeted by a chorus of applauding yells, and the crowd started up the levee. Half of the men in the crowd, and they were all of them young, were drunk.

Taylor, when seen at the charity hospital, was suffering greatly, and presented a pitiable spectacle. His clothing was covered with blood, and his face was beaten almost into a pulp. He said that he had gone to the market to work and was quietly sitting down when the mob came and began to fire on him. He was not aware at first that the crowd was after him. When he saw its purpose he tried to run, but fell. He didn't know any of the men in the crowd. There is hardly a chance that Taylor will recover.

The police told the crowd to move on, but no attempt was made to arrest anyone.

A GRAY-HAIRED VICTIM

The bloodthirsty barbarians, having tasted blood, continued their hunt and soon ran across an old man of seventy-five years. His life had been spent in hard work about the French market, and he was well known as an unoffending, peaceable and industrious old man.

But that made no difference to the mob. He was a Negro, and with a fiendishness that was worse than that of cannibals they beat his life out. The report says:

There was another gang of men parading the streets in the lower part of the city, looking for any stray Negro who might be on the streets. As they neared the corner of Dauphine and Kerlerec, a square below Esplanade Avenue, they came upon Baptiste Thilo, an aged Negro, who works in the French Market.

Thilo for years has been employed by the butchers and fish merchants to carry baskets from the stalls to the wagons, and unload the wagons as they arrive in the morning. He was on his way to the market, when the mob came upon him. One of the gang struck the old Negro, and as he fell, another in the crowd, supposed to be a young fellow, fired a shot. The bullet entered the body just below the right nipple.

As the Negro fell the crowd looked into his face and they discovered then that the victim was very old. The young man who did the shooting said: "Oh, he is an old Negro. I'm sorry that I shot him."

This is all the old Negro received in the way of consolation.

He was left where he fell, but later staggered to his feet and made his way to the third precinct station.

There the police summoned the ambulance and the students pronounced the wound very dangerous.

He was carried to the hospital as rapidly as possible.
There was no arrest.

Just before daybreak the mob found another victim. He, too, was on his way to market, driving a meat wagon. But little is told of his treatment, nothing more than the following brief statement:

At nearly 3 o'clock this morning a report was sent to the Third Precinct station that a Negro was lying on the sidewalk at the corner of Decatur and St. Philip. The man had been pulled off of a meat wagon and riddled with bullets.

When the police arrived he was insensible and apparently dying. The ambulance students attended the Negro and pronounced the wounds fatal.

There was nothing found which would lead to the discovery of his identity.

FUN IN GRETNA

If there are any persons so deluded as to think that human life in the South is valued any more than the life of a brute, he will be speedily undeceived by reading the accounts of unspeakable barbarism committed by the mob in and around New Orleans. In no other civilized country in the world, nay, more, in no land of barbarians would it be possible to duplicate the scenes of brutality that are reported from New Orleans. In the heat of blind fury one might conceive how a mad mob might beat and kill a man taken red-handed in a brutal murder. But it is almost past belief to read that civilized white people, men who boast of their chivalry and blue blood, actually had fun in beating, chasing and shooting men who had no possible connection with any crime.

But this actually happened in Gretna, a few miles from New Orleans. In its description of the scenes of Tuesday night, the *Picayune* mentions the brutal chase of several colored men whom the mob sought to kill. In the instances mentioned, the paper said:

> Gretna had its full share of excitement between 8 and 11 o'clock last night, in connection with a report that spread through the town that a Negro resembling the slayer of Police Captain Day, of New Orleans, had been seen on the outskirts of the place.
>
> It is true that a suspicious-looking Negro was observed by the residents of Madison and Amelia Streets lurking about the fences of that neighborhood just after dark, and shortly before 8 o'clock John Fist, a young white man, saw the Negro on Fourth Street. He followed the darkey a short distance, and, coming upon Robert Moore, who is known about town as the "black detective," Fist pointed the Negro

out and Moore at once made a move toward the stranger. The latter observed Moore making in his direction, and, without a word, he sped in the direction of the Brooklyn pasture, Moore following and firing several shots at him. In a few minutes a half hundred white men, including Chief of Police Miller, Constable Dannenhauer, Patrolman Keegan and several special officers, all well-armed, joined in the chase, but in the darkness the Negro escaped.

Just as the pursuing party reached town again, two of the residents of Lafayette Avenue, Peter Leson and Robert Henning, reported that they had just chased and shot at a Negro, who had been seen in the yard of the former's house. They were positive the Negro had not escaped from the square. Their report was enough to set the appetite of the crowd on edge, and the square was quickly surrounded, while several dozens of men, armed with lanterns and revolvers, made a search of every yard and under every house in the square. No Negro was found.

The crowd of armed men was constantly swelling, and at 10 o'clock it had reached the proportions of a small army. At 10:30 o'clock an outbound freight train is due to pass through Gretna on the Texas and Pacific Road, and the crowd, believing that Captain Day's slayer might be aboard one of the cars attempting to leave the scene of his crime, resolved to inspect the train. As the train stopped at the Madison Street crossing the engineer was requested to pull very slowly through the town, in order that the trucks of the cars might be examined. There was a string of armed men on each side of the railroad track and in a few moments a Negro was espied riding between two cars. A half dozen weapons were pointed at him and he was ordered to come out. He sprang out with alacrity and was pounced upon almost before he reached the ground. Robert Moore grabbed him and pushed an ugly-looking Derringer under his nose and the Negro threw up both hands. Constable Dannenhauer and Patrolman Keegan took charge of him and hustled him off to jail, where he was locked up. The Negro does not at all resemble Robert Charles, but it was best for his sake that he was placed under lock and key.

The crowd was not in a humor to let any Negro pass muster last night. The prisoner gave his name as Luke Wallace.

But now came the real excitement. The train had slowed down almost to a standstill, in the very heart of town. Somebody shouted: "There he goes, on top of the train!" And sure enough, somebody was going. It was a Negro, too, and he was making a bee-line for the front end of the train. A veritable shower of bullets, shot and rifle balls greeted the flying form, but on it sped. The locomotive had stopped in the middle of the square between La voisier and Newton Streets, and the Negro, flying with the speed of the wind along the top of the cars, reached the first car of the train and jumped to the tender and then into the cab. As he did several white men standing at the locomotive made a rush into the cab. The Negro sprang swiftly out of the other side, on to the sidewalk. But there were several more men, and as he realized that he was rushing right into their arms he made a spring to leap over the fence of Mrs. Linden's home, on the wood side of the track. Before the Negro got to the top one white man had hold of his legs, while another rushed up, pistol in hand. The man who was holding the darkey's legs was jostled out of the way and the man with the pistol, standing directly beneath the Negro, sent two bullets at him.

There was a wild scramble, and the vision of a fleeing form in the Linden yard, but that was the last seen of the black man. The yard was entered and searched, and neighboring yards were also searched, but not even the trace of blood was found. It is almost impossible to believe that the Negro was not wounded, for the man who fired at him held the pistol almost against the Negro's body.

The shots brought out almost everybody—white—in town, and though there was nothing to show for the exciting work, except the arrest of the Negro, who doesn't answer the description of the man wanted, Gretna's male population had its little fan and felt amply repaid for all the trouble it was put to, and all the ammunition it wasted.

BRUTALITY IN
NEW ORLEANS

Mob rule reigned supreme Wednesday, and the scenes that were enacted challenge belief. How many colored men and women were abused and injured is not known, for those who escaped were glad to make a place of refuge and took no time to publish their troubles. The mob made no attempt to find Charles; its only purpose was to pursue, beat and kill any colored man or woman who happened to come in sight. Speaking editorially, the *Picayune* of Thursday, the twenty-sixth of July, said:

Escaped with Their Lives

At the Charity Hospital Wednesday night more than a score of people were treated for wounds received at the hands of the mob. Some were able to tell of their mistreatment, and their recitals are briefly given in the *Picayune* as follows:

Alex. Ruffin, who is quite seriously injured, is a Pullman car porter, a native of Chicago. He reached New Orleans at 9:20 o'clock last night, and after finishing his work, boarded a Henry Clay Avenue car to go to Delachaise Street, where he has a sick son.

"I hadn't ridden any way," said he, "when I saw a lot of white folks. They were shouting to 'Get the Niggers.' I didn't know they were after every colored man they saw, and sat still. Two or three men jumped on the car and started at me. One of them hit me over the head with a slungshot, and they started to shooting at me. I jumped out of the car and ran, although I had done nothing. They shot me in the arm and in the leg. I would certainly have been killed had not some gentleman taken my part. If I had known New Orleans was so excited I would

never have left my car."

George Morris is the name of a Negro who was badly injured by a mob which went through the Poydras Market. Morris is employed as watchman there. He heard the noise of the passing crowd and looked out to see what the matter was. As soon as the mob saw him its members started after him.

"One man hit me over the head with a club," said George, after his wounds had been dressed, "and somebody cut me in the back. I didn't hardly think what was the matter at first, but when I saw they were after me I ran for my life. I ran to the coffee stand, where I work, for protection, but they were right after me, and somebody shot me in the back. At last the police got me away from the crowd. Just before I was hit a friend of mine, who was in the crowd, said, 'You had better go home, Nigger; they're after your kind.' I didn't know then what he meant. I found out pretty quick."

Morris is at the hospital. He is a perfect wreck, and while he will probably get well, he will have had a close call.

Esther Fields is a Negro washerwoman who lives at South Claiborne and Toledano Streets. She was at home when she heard a big noise and went out to investigate. She ran into the arms of the mob, and was beaten into insensibility in less time than it takes to tell it. Esther is being treated at the charity hospital, and should be able to get about in a few days. The majority of her bruises are about the head.

T.P. Sanders fell at the hands of the Jackson Avenue mob. He lives at 1927 Jackson Avenue, and was sitting in front of his home when he saw the crowd marching out the street. He stayed to see what the excitement was all about, and was shot in the knee and thorax and horribly beaten about the head before the mob came to the conclusion that he had been done for, and passed on. The ambulance was called and he was picked up and carried to the charity hospital, where his wounds were dressed and pronounced serious.

Oswald McMahon is nothing more than a boy. He was shot in the leg and afterward carried to the hospital. His injuries are very slight.

Dan White is another charity hospital patient. He is a Negro roustabout and was sitting in the bar room at Poydras and Franklin Streets when a mob passed along and espied him. He was shot in the hand, and would have been roughly dealt with had some policeman not been luckily near and rescued him.

In addition to the Negroes who suffered from the violence of the mob there were several patients treated at the hospital during the night who had been with the rioters and had been struck by stray bullets or injured in scuffles. None of this class were hurt to any extent. They got their wounds dressed and went out again.

WAS CHARLES
A DESPERADO?

The press of the country has united in declaring that Robert Charles was a desperado. As usual, when dealing with a negro, he is assumed to be guilty because he is charged. Even the most conservative of journals refuse to ask evidence to prove that the dead man was a criminal, and that his life had been given over to lawbreaking. The minute that the news was flashed across the country that he had shot a white man it was at once declared that he was a fiend incarnate, and that when he was killed the community would be ridden of a black-hearted desperado. The reporters of the New Orleans papers, who were in the best position to trace the record of this man's life, made every possible effort to find evidence to prove that he was a villain unhung. With all the resources at their command, and inspired by intense interest to paint him as black a villain as possible, these reporters signally failed to disclose a single indictment which charged Robert Charles with a crime. Because they failed to find any legal evidence that Charles was a lawbreaker and desperado his accusers gave full license to their imagination and distorted the facts that they had obtained, in every way possible, to prove a course of criminality, which the records absolutely refuse to show.

Charles had his first encounter with the police Monday night, in which he was shot in the street duel which was begun by the police after Officer Mora had beaten Charles three or four times over the head with his billy in an attempt to make an illegal arrest. In defending himself against the combined attack of two officers with a billy and their guns upon him, Charles shot

Officer Mora and escaped.

Early Tuesday morning Charles was traced to Dryades Street by officers who were instructed to kill him on sight. There, again defending himself, he shot and killed two officers. This, of course, in the eyes of the American press, made him a desperado. The New Orleans press, in substantiating the charges that he was a desperado, make statements which will be interesting to examine.

In the first place the *New Orleans Times-Democrat*, of July 25, calls Charles a "ravisher and a daredevil." It says that from all sources that could be searched "the testimony was cumulative that the character of the murderer, Robert Charles, is that of a daredevil and a fiend in human form." Then in the same article it says:

> The belongings of Robert Charles which were found in his room were a complete index to the character of the man. Although the room and its contents were in a state of chaos on account of the frenzied search for clews by officers and citizens, an examination of his personal effects revealed the mental state of the murderer and the rancor in his heart toward the Caucasian race. Never was the adage, "A little learning is a dangerous thing," better exemplified than in the case of the negro who shot to death the two officers.

His room was searched, and the evidence upon which the charge that he was a desperado consisted of pamphlets in support of Negro emigration to Liberia. On his mantel-piece there was found a bullet mold and an outfit for reloading cartridges. There were also two pistol scabbards and a bottle of cocaine. The other evidences that Charles was a desperado the writer described as follows:

> In his room were found negro periodicals and other "race" propaganda, most of which was in the interest of the negro's emigration to Liberia. There were Police Gazettes strewn about his

room and other papers of a similar character. Well-worn textbooks, bearing his name written in his own scrawling handwriting, and well-filled copybooks found in his trunk showed that he had burnt the midnight oil, and was desirous of improving himself intellectually in order that he might conquer the hated white race. Much of the literature found among his chattels was of a superlatively vituperative character, and attacked the white race in unstinted language and asserted the equal rights of the Negro.

Charles was evidently the local agent of the *Voice of Missions*, a "religious" paper, published at Atlanta, as great bundles of that sheet were found. It is edited by one Bishop Turner, and seems to be the official organ of all haters of the white race. Its editorials are anarchistic in the extreme, and urge upon the negro that the sooner he realizes that he is as good as the white man the better it will be for him. The following verses were clipped from the journal; they were marked "till forbidden," and appeared in several successive numbers:

OUR SENTIMENTS

H. M. T.

My country, 'tis of thee,
Dear land of Africa,
        Of thee we sing.
Land where our fathers died,
Land of the Negro's pride,
        God's truth shall ring.

My native country, thee,
Land of the black and free,
        Thy name I love;
To see thy rocks and rills,
Thy woods and matchless hills,
        Like that above.

63

When all thy slanderous ghouls,
In the bosom of sheol,
   Forgotten lie,
Thy monumental name shall live,
And suns thy royal brow shall gild,
Upheaved to heaven high,
   O'ertopping thrones.

There were no valuables in his room, and if he was a professional thief he had his headquarters for storing his plunder at some other place than his room on Fourth Street. Nothing was found in his room that could lead to the belief that he was a thief, except fifty or more small bits of soap. The inference was that every place he visited he took all of the soap lying around, as all of the bits were well worn and had seen long service on the washstand.

His wearing apparel was little more than rags, and financially he was evidently not in a flourishing condition. He was in no sense a skilled workman, and his room showed, in fact, that he was nothing more than a laborer.

The "philosopher in the garret" was a dirty wretch, and his room, his bedding and his clothing were nasty and filthy beyond belief. His object in life seemed to have been the discomfiture of the white race, and to this purpose he devoted himself with zeal. He declared himself to be a "patriot," and wished to be the Moses of his race.

Under the title of "The Making of a Monster," the reporter attempts to give "something of the personality of the archfiend, Charles." Giving his imagination full vent the writer says:

It is only natural that the deepest interest should attach to the personality of Robert Charles. What manner of man was this fiend incarnate? What conditions developed him? Who were his preceptors? From what ancestral strain, if any, did he derive his ferocious hatred of the whites, his cunning, his brute courage, the apostolic zeal which he displayed in spreading the propaganda of African equality? These are questions involving one of the most remarkable psychological problems of modern times.

In answer to the questions which he propounds, the reporter proceeds to admit that he did not learn anything of a very desperate nature connected with Charles. He says:

Although Charles was a familiar figure to scores of Negroes in New Orleans, and they had been more or less intimately acquainted with him for over two years, curiously little can be learned of his habits or mode of life. Since the perpetration of his terrible series of crimes it goes without saying that his former friends are inclined to be reticent, but it is reasonably certain that they have very little to tell. In regard to himself, Charles was singularly reticent for a Negro. He did not even indulge in the usual lying about his prowess and his adventures. This was possibly due to the knowledge that he was wanted for a couple of murders. The man had sense enough to know that it would be highly unwise to excite any curiosity about his past.

When Charles first came to New Orleans he worked here and there as a day laborer. He was employed at different times in a sawmill, on the street gangs, as a roustabout on the levee, as a helper at the sugar works and as a coal shoveler in the engine room of the St. Charles Hotel. At each of the places where he worked he was known as a quiet, rather surly fellow, who had little to say to anybody, and generally performed his tasks in morose silence. He managed to convey the impression, however, of being a man of more than ordinary intelligence.

A Negro named William Butts, who drives a team on the levee and lives on Washington Street, near Baronne, told a *Times-Democrat* reporter yesterday that Charles got a job about a year ago as agent for a Liberian Immigration Society, which has headquarters at Birmingham, and was much elated at the prospect of making a living without hard labor.

According to the further investigations of this reporter,

Charles was also agent for Bishop Turner's *Voice of Missions*, the colored missionary organ of the African Methodist Church, edited by H.M. Turner, of Atlanta, Georgia. Concerning his service as agent for the *Voice of Missions*, the reporter says:

> He secured a number of subscribers and visited them once a month to collect the installments. In order to insure regular payments it was necessary to keep up enthusiasm, which was prone to wane, and Charles consequently became an active and continual preacher of the propaganda of hatred. Whatever may have been his private sentiments at the outset, this constant harping on one string must eventually have had a powerful effect upon his own mind.
>
> Exactly how he received his remuneration is uncertain, but he told several of his friends that he got a "big commission." Incidentally he solicited subscribers for a Negro paper called the *Voice of the Missions*, and when he struck a Negro who did not want to go to Africa himself, he begged contributions for the "good of the cause."
>
> In the course of time Charles developed into a fanatic on the subject of the Negro oppression and neglected business to indulge in wild tirades whenever he could find a listener. He became more anxious to make converts than to obtain subscribers, and the more conservative darkies began to get afraid of him. Meanwhile he got into touch with certain agitators in the North and made himself a distributing agent for their literature, a great deal of which he gave away. Making money was a secondary consideration to "the cause."
>
> One of the most enthusiastic advocates of the Liberian scheme is the colored Bishop H.M. Turner, of Atlanta. Turner is a man of unusual ability, has been over to Africa personally several times, and has made himself conspicuous by denouncing laws which he claimed discriminated against the blacks. Charles was one of the bishop's disciples and evidence has been found that seems to indicate they were in correspondence.

This was all that the *Times-Democrat*'s reporters could find after the most diligent search to prove that Charles was the fiend incarnate which the press of New Orleans and elsewhere declared him to be.

The reporters of the *New Orleans Picayune* were no more successful than their brethren of the *Times-Democrat*. They, too, were compelled to substitute fiction for facts in their attempt to prove Charles a desperado. In the issue of the twenty-sixth of July it was said that Charles was well known in Vicksburg, and was there a consort of thieves. They mentioned that a man named Benson Blake was killed in 1894 or 1895, and that four Negroes were captured, and two escaped. Of the two escaped they claim that Charles was one. The four negroes who were captured were put in jail, and as usual, in the high state of civilization which characterizes Mississippi, the right of the person accused of crime to an indictment by legal process and a legal trial by jury was considered an useless formality if the accused happened to be black. A mob went to the jail that night, the four colored men were delivered to the mob, and all four were hanged in the court-house yard. The reporters evidently assumed that Charles was guilty, if, in fact, he was ever there, because the other four men were lynched. They did not consider it was a fact of any importance that Charles was never indicted. They called him a murderer on general principles.

DIED IN SELF-DEFENSE

The life, character and death of Robert Charles challenges the thoughtful consideration of all fair-minded people. In the frenzy of the moment, when nearly a dozen men lay dead, the victims of his unerring and death-dealing aim, it was natural for a prejudiced press and for citizens in private life to denounce him as a desperado and a murderer. But sea depths are not measured when the ocean rages, nor can absolute justice be determined while public opinion is lashed into fury. There must be calmness to insure correctness of judgment. The fury of the hour must abate before we can deal justly with any man or any cause.

That Charles was not a desperado is amply shown by the discussion in the preceding chapter. The darkest pictures which the reporters could paint of Charles were quoted freely, so that the public might find upon what grounds the press declared him to be a lawbreaker. Unquestionably the grounds are wholly insufficient. Not a line of evidence has been presented to prove that Charles was the fiend which the first reports of the New Orleans charge him to be.

Nothing more should be required to establish his good reputation, for the rule is universal that a reputation must be assumed to be good until it is proved bad. But that rule does not apply to the Negro, for as soon as he is suspected the public judgment immediately determines that he is guilty of whatever crime he stands charged. For this reason, as a matter of duty to the race, and the simple justice to the memory of Charles, an investigation has been made of the life and character of Charles before the fatal affray which led to his death.

Robert Charles was not an educated man. He was a student who faithfully investigated all the phases of oppression from which his race has suffered. That he was a student is amply shown by the *Times-Democrat* report of the twenty-fifth, which says:

"Well-worn textbooks, bearing his name written in his own scrawling handwriting, and well-filled copy-books found in his trunk, showed that he had burned the midnight oil, and desired to improve himself intellectually in order that he might conquer the hated white race."

From this quotation it will be seen that he spent the hours after days of hard toil in trying to improve himself, both in the study of textbooks and in writing.

He knew that he was a student of a problem which required all the intelligence that a man could command, and he was burning his midnight oil gathering knowledge that he might better be able to come to an intelligent solution. To his aid in the study of this problem he sought the aid of a Christian newspaper, the *Voice of Missions*, the organ of the African Methodist Episcopal Church. He was in communication with its editor, who is a bishop, and is known all over this country as a man of learning, a lover of justice and the defender of law and order. Charles could receive from Bishop Turner not a word of encouragement to be other than an earnest, tireless and God-fearing student of the complex problems which affected the race.

For further help and assistance in his studies, Charles turned to an organization which has existed and flourished for many years, at all times managed by men of high Christian standing and absolute integrity. These men believe and preach a doctrine that the best interests of the Negro will be subserved by an emigration from America back to the Fatherland, and they do all they can to spread the doctrine of emigration and to give material assistance to those who desire to leave America and make their future homes in Africa. This organization is known as "The International Migration Society." It has its headquarters in Birmingham, Alabama. From this place it issues pamphlets, some of which were found, in the home of Robert Charles, and which pamphlets the reporters of the New Orleans papers declare to be incendiary and dangerous in their doctrine and teaching.

Nothing could be further from the truth. Copies of any and all of them may be secured by writing to D.J. Flummer, who is President and in charge of the home office in Birmingham, Alabama. Three of the pamphlets found in Charles's room are named respectively:

First, *Prospectus of the Liberian Colonization Society*; which pamphlet in a few brief pages tells of the work of the society, plans, prices and terms of transportation of colored people who choose to go to Africa. These pages are followed by a short, conservative discussion of the Negro question, and close with an argument that Africa furnishes the best asylum for the oppressed Negroes in this country.

The second pamphlet is entitled *Christian Civilization of Africa*. This is a brief statement of the advantages of the Republic of Liberia, and an argument in support of the superior conditions which colored people may attain to by leaving the South and settling in Liberia.

The third pamphlet is entitled *The Negro and Liberia*. This is a larger document than the other two, and treats more exhaustively the question of emigration, but from the first page to the last there is not an incendiary line or sentence. There is not even a suggestion of violence in all of its thirty-two pages, and not a word which could not be preached from every pulpit in the land.

If it is true that the workman is known by his tools, certainly no harm could ever come from the doctrines which were preached by Charles or the papers and pamphlets distributed by him. Nothing ever written in the *Voice of Missions*, and nothing ever published in the pamphlets above alluded to in the remotest way suggest that a peaceable man should turn lawbreaker, or that any man should dye his hands in his brother's blood.

70

In order to secure as far as possible positive information about the life and character of Robert Charles, it was plain that the best course to pursue was to communicate with those with whom he had sustained business relations. Accordingly a letter was forwarded to Mr. D.J. Flummer, who is president of the colonization society, in which letter he was asked to state in reply what information he had of the life and character of Robert Charles. The result was a very prompt letter in response, the text of which is as follows:

Birmingham, Ala.,
Aug. 21, 1900

MRS. IDA B. WELLS BARNETT, *Chicago*, Ill.:

Dear Madam—Replying to your favor of recent date requesting me to write you giving such information as I may have concerning the life, habits and character of Robert Charles, who recently shot and killed police officers in New Orleans, I wish to say that my knowledge of him is only such as I have gained from his business connection with the International Migration Society during the past five or six years, during which time I was president of the society.

He having learned that the purpose of this society was to colonize the colored people in Liberia, West Africa, and thereby lessen or destroy the friction and prejudice existing in this country between the two races, set about earnestly and faithfully distributing the literature that we issued from time to time. He always appeared to be mild but earnest in his advocacy of emigration, and never to my knowledge used any method or means that would in the least appear unreasonable, and had always kept within the bounds of law and order in advocating emigration.

The work he performed for this society was all gratuitous, and apparently prompted from his love of humanity, and desires to be instrumental in building up a Negro Nationality in Africa. If he ever violated a law before the killing of the policemen, I do not know of it.

Yours, very truly,

D. J. Flummer

Besides this statement, Mr. Flummer enclosed a letter received by the Society two days before the tragedy at New Orleans. This letter was written by Robert Charles, and it attests his devotion to the cause of emigration which he had espoused. Memoranda on the margin of the letter show that the order was filled by mailing the pamphlets. It is very probable that these were the identical pamphlets which were found by the mob which broke into the room of Robert Charles and seized upon these harmless documents and declared they were sufficient evidence to prove Charles a desperado. In the light of subsequent events the letter of Charles, which follows, sounds like a voice from the tomb:

New Orleans,
July 30,1900

Mr. D. J. Flummer:

Dear Sir—I received your last pamphlets and they are all given out. I want you to send me some more, and I enclose you the stamps. I think I will go over in Greenville, Miss., and give my people some pamphlets over there.

Yours truly,

Robert Charles

The latest word of information comes from New Orleans from a man who knew Charles intimately for six years. For obvious reasons, his name is withheld. In answer to a letter sent him he answers as follows:

New Orleans,
Aug. 23, 1900

Mrs. Ida B. Wells-Barnett: /

Dear Madam—It affords me great pleasure to inform you as far as I know of Robert Charles. I have been acquainted with him about six years in this city. He never has, as I know, given any trouble to anyone. He was quiet and a peaceful man and was very frank in speaking. He was too much of a hero to die; few call be found to equal him. I am very sorry to say that I do not know anything of his birthplace, nor his parents, but enclosed find letter from his uncle, from which you may find more information. You will also find one of the circulars in which Charles was in possession of which was styled as a crazy document. Let me say, until our preachers preach this document we will always be slaves. If you can help circulate this "crazy" doctrine I would be glad to have you do so, for I shall never rest until I get to that heaven on earth; that is, the west coast of Africa, in Liberia.

With best wishes to you I still remain, as always, for the good of the race,

By only those whose anger and vindictiveness warp their judgment is Robert Charles a desperado. Their word is not supported by the statement of a single fact which justifies their judgment and no criminal record shows that he was ever indicted for any offense, much less convicted of crime. On the contrary, his work for many years had been with Christian people, circulating emigration pamphlets and active as agent for a mission publication. Men who knew him say that he was a law-abiding, quiet, industrious, peaceable man. So he lived.

So he lived and so he would have died had not he raised his hand to resent unprovoked assault and unlawful arrest that fateful Monday night. That made him an outlaw, and being a man of courage he decided to die with his face to the foe. The white people of this country may charge that he was a desperado, but to the people of his own race Robert Charles will always be regarded as the hero of New Orleans.

BURNING
HUMAN BEINGS ALIVE

Not only has life been taken by mobs in the past twenty years, but the ordinary procedure of hanging and shooting have been improved upon during the past ten years. Fifteen human beings have been burned to death in the different parts of the country by mobs. Men, women and children have gone to see the sight, and all have approved the barbarous deeds done in the high light of the civilization and Christianity of this country.

In 1891 Ed Coy was burned to death in Texarkana, Ark. He was charged with assaulting a white woman, and after the mob had securely tied him to a tree, the men and boys amused themselves for some time sticking knives into Coy's body and slicing off pieces, of flesh. When they had amused themselves sufficiently, they poured coal oil over him and the women in the case set fire to him. It is said that fifteen thousand people stood by and saw him burned. This was on a Sunday night, and press reports told how the people looked on while the Negro burned to death.

Feb. 1, 1893, Henry Smith was burned to death in Paris, Texas. The entire county joined in that exhibition. The district attorney himself went for the prisoner and turned him over to the mob. He was placed upon a float and drawn by four white horses through the principal streets of the city. Men, women and children stood at their doors and waved their handkerchiefs and cheered the echoes. They knew that the man was to be burned to death because the newspaper had declared for three days previous that this would be so. Excursions were run by all the railroads, and the mayor of the town gave the children a holiday so that they might see the sight.

Henry Smith was charged with having assaulted and murdered a little white girl. He was an imbecile, and while he had killed the child, there was no proof that he had criminally assaulted her. He was tied to a stake on a platform which had been built ten feet high, so that everybody might see the sight. The father and brother and uncle of the little white girl that had been murdered was upon that platform about fifty minutes entertaining the crowd of ten thousand persons by burning the victim's flesh with red-hot irons. Their own newspapers told how they burned his eyes out and, ran the red-hot iron down his throat, cooking his tongue, and how the crowd cheered wild delight. At last, having declared themselves satisfied, coal oil was poured over him and he was burned to death, and the mob fought over the ashes for bones and pieces of his clothes.

July 7, 1893, in Bardwell, Ky., C.J. Miller was burned to ashes. Since his death this man has been found to be absolutely innocent of the murder of the two white girls with which he was charged. But the mob would wait for no justification. They insisted that, as they were not sure he was the right man, they would compromise the matter by hanging him instead of burning. Not to be outdone, they took the body down and made a huge bonfire out of it.

July 22, 1893, at Memphis, Tenn., the body of Lee Walker was dragged through the street and burned before the court house. Walker had frightened some girls in a wagon along a country road by asking them to let him ride in their wagon. They cried out; some men working in a field near by said it was at attempt of assault, and of course began to look for their prey. There was never any charge of rape; the women only declared that he attempted an assault. After he was apprehended and put in jail and perfectly helpless, the mob dragged him out, shot him, cut him, beat him with sticks, built a fire and burned the legs off, then took the trunk of the body down and dragged further up the street, and at last burned it before the court house.

Sept. 20, 1893, at Roanoke, Va., the body of a Negro who had quarreled with a white woman was burned in the presence of several thousand persons. These people also wreaked their vengeance upon this helpless victim of the mob's wrath by sticking knives into him, kicking him and beating him with stones and otherwise mutilating him before life was extinct.

June 11, 1898, at Knoxville, Ark., James Perry was shut up in a cabin because he had smallpox and burned to death. He had been quarantined in this cabin when it was declared that he had this disease and the doctor sent for. When the physician arrived he found only a few smoldering embers. Upon inquiry some railroad hands who were working nearby revealed the fact that they had fastened the door of the cabin and set fire to the cabin and burned man and hut together.

Feb. 22, 1898, at Lake City, S.C., Postmaster Baker and his infant child were burned to death by a mob that had set fire to his house. Mr. Baker's crime was that he had refused to give up the post office, to which he had been appointed by the National Government. The mob had tried to drive him away by persecution and intimidation. Finding that all else had failed, they went to his home in the dead of night and set fire to his house, and as the family rushed forth they were greeted by a volley of bullets. The father and his baby were shot through the open door and wounded so badly that they fell back in the fire and were burned to death. The remainder of the family, consisting of the wife and five children, escaped with their lives from the burning house, but all of them were shot, one of the number made a cripple for life.

Jan. 7, 1898, two Indians were tied to a tree at Maud Post Office, Indian Territory, and burned to death by a white mob. They were charged with murdering a white woman. There was no proof of their guilt except the unsupported word of the mob. Yet they were tied to a tree and slowly roasted to death. Their names were Lewis McGeesy and Hond Martin. Since that time these boys have been found to be absolutely innocent of the charge. Of course that discovery is too late to be of any benefit to them, but because they were Indians the Indian Commissioner demanded and received from the United States Government an indemnity of $13,000.

April 23, 1899, at Palmetto, Ga., Sam Hose was burned alive in the presence of a throng, on Sunday afternoon. He was charged with killing a man named Cranford, his employer, which he admitted he did because his employer was about to shoot him. To the fact of killing the employer was added the absolutely false charge that Hose assaulted the wife. Hose was arrested and no trial was given him. According to the code of reasoning of the mob, none was needed. A white man had been killed and a white woman was said to have been assaulted. That was enough. When Hose was found he had to die.

The Atlanta Constitution, in speaking of the murder of Cranford, said that the Negro who was suspected would be burned alive. Not only this, but it offered $500 reward for his capture. After he had been apprehended, it was publicly announced that he would be burned alive. Excursion trains were run and bulletins were put up in the small towns. The Governor of Georgia was in Atlanta while excursion trains were being made up to take visitors to the burning. Many fair ladies drove out in their carriages on Sunday afternoon to witness the torture and burning of a human being. Hose's ears were cut off, then his toes and fingers, and passed round to the crowd. His eyes were put out, his tongue torn out and flesh cut in strips by knives. Finally they poured coal oil on him and burned him to death. They dragged his half-consumed trunk out of the flames, cut it open, extracted his heart and liver, and sold slices for ten cents each for souvenirs, all of which was published most promptly in the daily papers of Georgia and boasted over by the people of that section.

Oct. 19, 1889, at Canton, Miss., Joseph Leflore was burned to death. A house had been entered and its occupants murdered during the absence of the husband and father. When the discovery was made, it was immediately supposed that the crime was the work of a Negro, and the motive that of assaulting white women.

Bloodhounds were procured and they made a round of the village and discovered only one colored man absent from his home. This was taken to be proof sufficient that he was the perpetrator of the deed. When he returned home he was apprehended, taken into the yard of the house that had been burned down, tied to a stake, and was slowly roasted to death.

Dec. 6, 1899, at Maysville, Ky., Wm. Coleman also was burned to death. He was slowly roasted, first one foot and then the other, and dragged out of the fire so that the torture might be prolonged. All of this without a shadow of proof or scintilla of evidence that the man had committed the crime.

Thus have the mobs of this country taken the lives of their victims within the past ten years. In every single instance except one these burnings were witnessed by from two thousand to fifteen thousand people, and no one person in all these crowds throughout the country had the courage to raise his voice and speak out against the awful barbarism of burning human beings to death.

Men and women of America, are you proud of this record which the Anglo-Saxon race has made for itself? Your silence seems to say that you are. Your silence encourages a continuance of this sort of horror. Only by earnest, active, united endeavor to arouse public sentiment can we hope to put a stop to these demonstrations of American barbarism.

LYNCHING RECORD

The following table of lynchings has been kept year by year by the Chicago Tribune, beginning with 1882, and shows the list of Negroes that have been lynched during that time:

1882, Negroes murdered by mobs 52
1883, Negroes murdered by mobs 39
1884, Negroes murdered by mobs 53
1885, Negroes murdered by mobs 164
1886, Negroes murdered by mobs 136
1887, Negroes murdered by mobs 128
1888, Negroes murdered by mobs 143
1889, Negroes murdered by mobs 127
1890, Negroes murdered by mobs 171
1891, Negroes murdered by mobs 192
1892, Negroes murdered by mobs 241
1893, Negroes murdered by mobs 200
1894, Negroes murdered by mobs 190
1895, Negroes murdered by mobs 171
1896, Negroes murdered by mobs 131
1897, Negroes murdered by mobs 156
1898, Negroes murdered by mobs 127
1899, Negroes murdered by mobs 107

Of these thousands of men and women who have been put to death without judge or jury, less than one-third of them have been even accused of criminal assault. The world at large has accepted unquestionably the statement that Negroes are lynched only for assaults upon white women. Of those who were lynched from 1882 to 1891, the first ten years of the tabulated lynching record, the charges are as follows:

Two hundred and sixty-nine were charged with rape; 253 with murder; 44 with robbery; 37 with incendiarism; 4 with burglary; 27 with race prejudice; 13 quarreled with white men; 10 with making threats; 7 with rioting; 5 with miscegenation; in 32 cases no reasons were given, the victims were lynched on general principles.

During the past five years the record is as follows:

Of the 171 persons lynched in 1895 only 34 were charged with this crime. In 1896, out of 131 persons who were lynched, only 34 were said to have assaulted women. Of the 156 in 1897, only 32. In 1898, out of 127 persons lynched, 24 were charged with the alleged "usual crime." In 1899, of the 107 lynchings, 16 were said to be for crimes against women. These figures, of course, speak for themselves, and to the unprejudiced, fair-minded person it is only necessary to read and study them in order to show that the charge that the Negro is a moral outlaw is a false one, made for the purpose of injuring the Negro's good name and to create public sentiment against him.

If public sentiment were alive, as it should be upon the subject, it would refuse to be longer hoodwinked, and the voice of conscience would refuse to be stilled by these false statements. If the laws of the country were obeyed and respected by the white men of the country who charge that the Negro has no respect for law, these things could not be, for every individual, no matter what the charge, would have a fair trial and an opportunity to prove his guilt or innocence before a tribunal of law.

That is all the Negro asks—that is all the friends of law and order need to ask, for once the law of the land is supreme, no individual who commits crime will escape punishment.

Individual Negroes commit crimes the same as do white men, but that the Negro race is peculiarly given to assault upon women, is a falsehood of the deepest dye. The tables given above show that the Negro who is saucy to white men is lynched as well as the Negro who is charged with assault upon women.

Less than one-sixth of the lynchings last year, 1899, were charged with rape.

The Negro points to his record during the war in rebuttal of this false slander. When the white women and children of the South had no protector save only these Negroes, not one instance is known where the trust was betrayed. It is remarkably strange that the Negro had more respect for womanhood with the white men of the South hundreds of miles away, than they have today, when surrounded by those who take their lives with impunity and burn and torture, even worse than the "unspeakable Turk."

Again, the white women of the North came South years ago, threaded the forests, visited the cabins, taught the schools and associated only with the Negroes whom they came to teach, and had no protectors near at hand. They had no charge or complaint to make of the danger to themselves after association with this class of human beings. Not once has the country been shocked by such recitals from them as come from the women who are surrounded by their husbands, brothers, lovers and friends. If the Negro's nature is bestial, it certainly should have proved itself in one of these two instances. The Negro asks only justice and an impartial consideration of these facts.

Made in the USA
Monee, IL
20 July 2022

10052302R00049